T000670S

PEARLS SEEKS
ENLIGHTENMENT

Other *Pearls Before Swine* Collections

Floundering Fathers
I Scream, You Scream, We All Scream Because Puns Suck
Stephan's Web
I'm Only in This for Me
King of the Comics
Breaking Stephan
Rat's Wars
Unsportsmanlike Conduct
Because Sometimes You Just Gotta Draw a Cover with Your Left Hand
Larry in Wonderland
When Pigs Fly
50,000,000 Pearls Fans Can't Be Wrong
The Saturday Evening Pearls
Macho Macho Animals
The Sopratos
Da Brudderhood of Zeeba Zeeba Eata
The Ratvolution Will Not Be Televised
Nighthogs
This Little Piggy Stayed Home
BLTs Taste So Darn Good

Treasuries

Pearls Awaits the Tide
Pearls Goes Hollywood
Pearls Takes a Wrong Turn
Pearls Hogs the Road
Pearls Gets Sacrificed
Pearls Falls Fast
Pearls Freaks the #%# Out*
Pearls Blows Up
Pearls Sells Out
The Crass Menagerie
Lions and Tigers and Crocs, Oh My!
Sgt. Piggy's Lonely Hearts Club Comic

Gift Books

Friends Should Know When They're Not Wanted
Da Crockydile Book o' Frendsheep

Kids' Books

Suit Your Selfie
When Crocs Fly
Skip School, Fly to Space
The Croc Ate My Homework
Beginning Pearls

PEARLS SEEKS ENLIGHTENMENT

Stephan Pastis

A *Pearls Before Swine* Treasury

Andrews McMeel
PUBLISHING®

Pearls Before Swine is distributed internationally by Andrews McMeel Syndication.

Pearls Seeks Enlightment copyright © 2023 by Stephan Pastis. All rights reserved. Printed in China. No part of this book may be used or reproduced in any manner whatsoever without written permission except in the case of reprints in the context of reviews.

Andrews McMeel Publishing
a division of Andrews McMeel Universal
1130 Walnut Street, Kansas City, Missouri 64106

www.andrewsmcmeel.com

23 24 25 26 27 SDB 10 9 8 7 6 5 4 3 2 1

ISBN: 978-1-5248-7924-2

Library of Congress Control Number: 2022947488

Pearls Before Swine can be viewed on the internet at www.pearlscomic.com.

These strips appeared in newspapers from March 30, 2020, to October 10, 2021.

Editor: Lucas Wetzel
Creative Director: Julie Phillips
Photographer: Ryan Schude
Cover Design: Donna Oatney
Text Design: Brittany Lee

Production Manager: Chuck Harper
Production Editor: Julie Railsback

ATTENTION: SCHOOLS AND BUSINESSES

Andrews McMeel books are available at quantity discounts with bulk purchase for educational, business, or sales promotional use. For information, please e-mail the Andrews McMeel Publishing Special Sales Department: sales@amuniversal.com.

Dedication

**In memory of my Dad,
Tom Pastis**

Introduction

Somewhere in the midst of the many pandemic lockdowns, I snapped.

I was bored of the routine. Desperate to see new things.

So I got in my car and drove.

One trip from Missouri to North Dakota, another from Oklahoma to Arkansas, and another from Delaware to Vermont. And through all of the many states in between.

But my favorite of all was my drive through the American Southwest—specifically, Arizona and New Mexico.

It covered all the places you'd expect, from Sedona (pictured above) to the Grand Canyon to Monument Valley, and then on through Navajo country to New Mexico, starting in Taos, and then south to Sante Fe, Albuquerque, and White Sands National Monument. I even stopped briefly near Los Alamos National Laboratory, in the hope that someone would share the secret of building an atomic bomb. But no one would help.

And so I left the uncooperative people of New Mexico and moved on to El Paso, Texas, where—if I had been given the atomic secrets—I was planning to cross the Rio Grande, sell the information to the Mexican government and disappear into a Mezcal-soaked retirement.

But that didn't happen.

So I decided to go with Plan B, which is to one day turn this and my other journeys into a travel book.

And when you want to do that, it means taking a slightly different route than the one you would normally take. Such as driving the backroads, and sometimes going out of your way to see things you might not otherwise see (I'm looking at you, World's Second Largest Garden Gnome.)

And it also means sitting down with locals and listening to what they have to say. From waitresses to priests, junkyard dealers to booksellers, bartenders to doctors.

So that's what I did.

And each day when I would get back to my hotel room, I would write down as much of it as I could.

Like the line from a parking lot attendant in Sedona who told me, "The vortex will heal your pain."

And the Navajo man who warned me, "Your car's too nice for these parts."

And the waitress in a small town cafe who said, "This town's not worth sh#t." (Which has always struck me as an odd expression given that I don't think anyone but a cattle farmer offers sh#t in exchange for anything.)

And so on the drive home from Texas, I decided to take one of those backroads I mentioned, in this case the little-known Highway 9, which for a good chunk of its lonely length runs right along the Mexican border, so close you can see the fence.

And there, in the company of tumbleweeds and border agents, I had a glorious epiphany:

I needed to go to the bathroom.

But this backroad traversed a land of snakes and cacti, not Starbucks and Chevrons, and there were no bathrooms in sight.

And before you say I should have just pulled over and stood by the side of the road like a manly man, let me confess right here that what I had to do was not, as my mother would say, "Number one." And this being the era of Instagram, I did not want to see myself tagged in a post labeled, "Cartoonist Stephan Pastis sh#tting on the highway."

And so I drove like a man possessed.

Until finally, God set before me a town.

If that's what one can call two buildings and a dog.

But the sign on one of those buildings read, "Tavern and Grill." Meaning that I could rush in, sprint for the bathroom, and if anyone asked questions, offer to buy everything on the menu twice.

Because that's what classy cartoonists do.

And so I walked up to the front door. But it was locked.

For despite this being the middle of the day, it was closed.

And let me use this moment to state one of the fundamental laws of human biology. That being this:

If you're racing for a bathroom and then learn you don't have access to that bathroom, it is a tragic event —for your innards have sensed the bathroom as well, and have given the alert to all appropriate organs that it is "all systems go." So if your urgency was previously at a 10 out of 10, that urgency has—like the amplifiers in Spinal Tap—somehow gone to 11.

And so it is no exaggeration to say that I sprinted for the building next door, a cinderblock cube with a blue wooden door that clearly had not been opened since the time of Geronimo.

But like the madman I had become, I knocked anyway. On the door, and even the windows, yelling, "IS THERE ANYONE IN THERE?!" so loud that I scared the lone dog, who startled and fled. Around the cinderblock building toward a second building behind it.

One I had not seen.

With a door. That was open.

And so, like that dog, I ran. Straight for the door. Stopping briefly in the open doorway, panting, sweating, staring, for before me was a human. Who, for all I cared, could have been Charles Manson fresh from the grave, and I still would have asked to use his bathroom.

"Can I help you?" asked the gray-haired man in jeans and denim shirt, who looked as startled to see me as I was to see him.

And looking around, I noticed for the first time that I was standing in, of all things, an art gallery.

An *art gallery.*

In a town with no post office, no gas stations, no cafes, no stores, one closed restaurant, and almost no people, I was face-to-face with a man who had the worst business plan in North America.

"I'm looking to buy art," I lied. "But first, could I use the bathroom?"

"It's really not for customers," he said, as though his permission mattered. As though he was talking to a normal man, and not a desperate one who was a split second away from shoving him aside and ripping the bathroom door off its hinges.

"But I guess you can use it," he added.

And so he led me through a door to the back room and said something about how to flush the toilet, and how not to do this, and how to be careful of blah blah blah—none of which I heard, for by that time I was in the bathroom doing what had to be done.

And walking out a new man, I headed back through the door to the gallery, offered the man my gratitude, and headed for the front door.

Completely forgetting my cover story.

Which was that I was a customer, and not just some guy using his place like a truckstop. And so, I stopped. And turned around. And took a moment to look at each of the dozen or so paintings he had on the walls.

"My wife wants something for our living room," I said, hoping to further cement my performance as a bona fide customer. "But these aren't quite her color scheme."

I smiled, hoping he wouldn't ask me what the phrase "color scheme" meant, as I didn't know. "Thank you, anyways," I added.

And he smiled back, but didn't answer.

And as I walked to my car, I felt bad.

Not bad-enough-to-buy-a-painting bad, but bad enough to do something. Like maybe give him some cash.

So I opened the glove compartment of the car and took out my wallet. Only to find there was no cash inside.

And that's when I saw what was lying on the back seat of the car.

An extra copy of my last treasury, *Pearls Awaits the Tide*.

Just waiting for a moment like this.

Just waiting to be given as a gift to a man who had surely never before met a syndicated cartoonist.

And so I grabbed the book and strutted back inside the gallery.

"Hey," I said. "I just want to give you this."

"What is it?" he asked.

"It's a *Pearls Before Swine* book."

He stared at the book in my hands.

"I'm the creator," I added, saving the best part for last.

And this was the moment where, at least in my mind, he would tell me that he was a subscriber to the local newspaper and loved the comic section, particularly *Pearls Before Swine*, and he couldn't believe I was standing in his gallery.

But instead he said:

"Why are you giving this to me?"

"To thank you."

He took the book from my hands and stared at it. "It's a cartoon?"

"Yeah, a comic strip. It's in a lot of newspapers. All around the country."

"I don't really read cartoons."

"Oh," I said, not quite expecting his reaction. "Well, maybe you can give it to somebody who does."

He thought about that. "I don't really know anyone who'd be interested. No offense. I mean, there's not many people out here."

And then he held out the book for me to take back.

"No, really," I said. "You keep it."

"You take it," he said.

"No, you take it," I said, as though my book was suddenly a radioactive potato.

And soon he sensed that the same man he didn't want entering his gallery would not be exiting his gallery if he did not just take the stupid book.

And so he took a deep breath and flipped through the pages with the same level of excitement a kid would show a molecular biology textbook.

"Listen," I said, "you were nice enough to let me use your bathroom. I'd feel bad if I didn't give you something back."

"Fine," he said, keeping the book. Until the moment I left, at which point he would see if it could serve as a doorstop, and if not, fling it into the unforgiving desert.

And that's when it hit me.

Not the book.

But the line from the waitress in that small town cafe.

The line that had never made sense.

"This town's not worth sh#t."

Only now it made sense.

I was trying to pay this man back for the use of his bathroom.

With my book.

Which wasn't worth sh#t.

Stephan Pastis
May 2023

Grab a cup of Arrivederci Bella A Cappella and join me for another treasury filled with my almost-never-enlightening commentary. (And I'm really hoping those Italian words don't translate to something obscene. If they do, I apologize on behalf of my editor.)

There's a recent photo of me during a beer-soaked vacation where my stomach had gotten so large it appeared I was with child.

15

HEY, GOAT, DID YOU SEE THAT THE LOTTO JACKPOT IS UP TO ALMOST ONE BILLION DOLLARS? IT'S CRAZY. SO I WENT OUT AND BOUGHT A HUNDRED DOLLARS' WORTH OF LOTTERY TICKETS.

PIG, THE ODDS OF THAT $100 WINNING YOU ONE BILLION DOLLARS ARE ABOUT THE SAME AS IF YOU HAD JUST BURIED IT IN THE GROUND.

I'LL TRY ANYTHING.

A neighbor of mine recently dug in his backyard and discovered an old gas station sign worth hundreds of dollars. So I started digging in my yard and found two scorpions.

WHAT ARE YOU DOING, PIG?

CREATING THE HAPPINESS CALENDAR.

WHAT IS IT?

IT'S LIKE A REGULAR CALENDAR, BUT ON EACH DAY, I INCLUDE SOMETHING IN LIFE THAT YOU CAN BE HAPPY ABOUT.

YOU'VE WRITTEN 'CHEESE' ON EVERY SINGLE DAY.

IT'S A KEY PART OF THE HAPPINESS CALENDAR.

HEY, RAT, WHAT ARE YOU DOING HERE?... I THOUGHT YOU WORKED TODAY.

I'M TELECOMMUTING. EVERYONE'S DOING IT. IT'S EFFICIENT AND TAKES ONE MORE CAR OFF THE ROAD.

THAT'S GREAT.

WAIT. AREN'T YOU A BARISTA?

I SAID MAKE IT YOURSELF, YOU PUTZ.

PERHAPS TELECOMMUTING CAN BE ABUSED.

I believe there were at least a couple of newspapers that wouldn't run this—apparently because there is a definition of "putz" that is not appropriate for newspapers. And when I say "apparently," I mean I knew that and wanted to see if I could get away with it.

I like doing strips like this where I know certain newspaper readers will read the first panel and start thinking about writing an angry letter to the editor, only to then discover in the second-to-last panel that the strip has a whole different meaning.

So I really was on vacation by myself in Medellín, Colombia, when the whole world shut down due to Covid in March of 2020, and I quickly found myself scrambling for the first flight home. Which was smart, because next door in Peru, the government stopped people from entering OR exiting, stranding numerous Americans for weeks.

While I did in fact have my drawing supplies with me, I thought it would be fun to try drawing these strips with pencil on a legal pad.

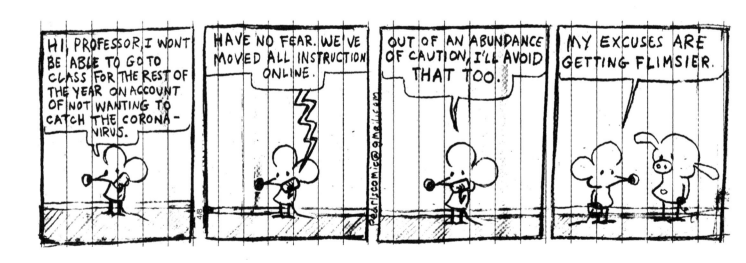

Because I usually work so far ahead and submit my strips roughly seven or eight months ahead of publication (i.e., a strip you see in December was probably created in April), being topical can be a bit tough. But there was no way I could avoid commenting on what was going on around us regarding Covid. So starting with this week of strips, I found myself constantly substituting out strips I'd already submitted and replacing them with these Covid-related ones.

After doing this strip, I discovered I had actually done almost this exact same strip before. I'll blame Covid, which I didn't have, but it sounds better than telling you I'm old.

I like that first panel of Pig just being sad. And that brings up an important point about this commentary: From time to time, I'll compliment myself and there's nothing you can do to stop me.

This was drawn when we were all trapped at home and coming to terms with what that was going to mean in our lives. For me, the only day-to-day change was that I stopped writing in cafés and stopped flying to Medellín, Colombia.

One of the aspects of the pandemic that will be the hardest for future generations to understand is how we all made a rush for toilet paper. I remember being thrilled if I went to the grocery store and saw some on the shelves, marking the first time in my life that I ever experienced joy in the toilet paper aisle.

This was one of the most popular strips of the year.

I don't play *Candy Crush*, but I *do* play far too much *Boggle With Friends*, a game where you try to make as many words as you can out of random letters in two minutes. I don't want to brag, but it may be my greatest skill in life.

ASHLEY'S LIFE

← Ashley

Get up every day before she wants to.

Is it 6:30 already?

ERRRR ERRR ERR

Sit in traffic for hours.

Beep! HONK! HONK!
Beep!

Go to a crappy job she dreads.

You are all morons.

Take kids everywhere always.

I'll be late for tennis!

I'll be late for soccer!

Look forward to that one week of vacation.

4/19

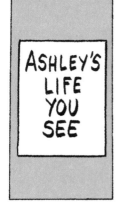

ASHLEY'S LIFE YOU SEE

ashley ...

#partyeveryday #beachlife
#livingmybestlife #cancun

ASHLEY HAS THE GREATEST LIFE.

HOW DOES SHE DO IT?

This was drawn in early April of the pandemic when deaths first began to skyrocket and we were all starting to realize what we were up against.

Pig is sort of the perfect character in tough times because he can project optimism in a way none of my other characters really can.

This was another really popular strip, because I think it's how everyone was feeling whenever they turned on the news.

Technically, you're supposed to put the little accents on the word "résumé," but it always looks distracting to me, so I don't do it. Plus, I don't think doing it my way causes any confusion. You may now resume reading the other comments.

I recently spoke via Zoom to a retirement home and really found out how true this was. I was supposed to be talking to them about my strip, but the people I talked to had such interesting pasts that I found myself just asking them questions.

For the life of me, I'll never understand how companies don't realize how maddening the repetition of their hold music can be. It's bad enough to be on hold. But it's torture listening to their #%#@%#$ song for the 100th time.

Even the crocs were thwarted by Covid restrictions.

I somehow failed to add the dot shading to the grass here, which is such a big mistake I can't believe I missed it. It would be like walking out the front door in the morning and forgetting to wear pants.

Which I've also done.

Okay, this is really me, except for the part where the guy's wife insists that he go to the party. My wife, Staci, is too smart for that and knows it's best if I stay home.

Panel 1: IN OTHER NEWS TODAY, PEOPLE EVERYWHERE BEGAN HOARDING MORE ITEMS.

Panel 2: THIS TIME, BOOKS... INTELLIGENT BOOKS... ON HISTORY, SCIENCE, THE ARTS...

Panel 3: RAISING THE COLLECTIVE I.Q. OF SO MANY PEOPLE THAT —

Panel 5: THE HOPEFUL DREAMS ARE THE WORST.

Feel free to hoard my *Pearls* books, *Timmy Failure* books, and *Trubble Town* books. Which is my way of shamelessly promoting every book series I've ever done.

Panel 1: Plusses and Minuses of getting out of bed this morning:

Panel 2: Minuses
- Cold floor
- Cold room
- No more pillow
- No more blankets
- Sleep done
- Responsibilities begin

Panel 3: Plusses

Panel 4: zzzzzzz

Panel 1: TIRED OF NOT GOING OUT? WELL, KISS THAT FEAR GOODBYE.

Panel 2: INTRODUCING THE BUBBLE 2000! GERM-PROOF! LEAK-PROOF! AND MOBILE AS ALL GET-OUT.
Germ-carrier → | Me ↓ | Germ-carrier →
Bubble 2000

Panel 3: AND BEST OF ALL, FOR THOSE DAYS YOU'RE NOT FEELING PARTICULARLY SOCIAL...

Panel 4: NIGHT MODE!
I THOUGHT I SAW RAT.
I DON'T SEE ANYONE.

Some reader reminded me during the pandemic that I actually had a character that was perfect for what was happening. Her name was Farina and she was a germophobic pig that lived in a germproof bubble. But because I had created her so long ago (2002), I totally forgot. Here is what she looked like:

Like many people during the pandemic, we got a new dog. We named her Total, in honor of the polar bear in my *Timmy Failure* series. And now I have to include a photo of her as a puppy:

I could not include Zebra in the Happy Box here as Larry the Croc would have eaten him, thereby changing the mood of the Happy Box.

This really is true. And dammit, I'm not there yet. And if I am, act surprised anyway.

I'm currently planning a trip where I drive all around Wisconsin. I'll let you know if I find any cheese dropping from the sky.

Somehow my farmer looks more like a repairman. Perhaps I should try drawing a repairman and see if he looks like a farmer.

5/17

The year 2020 had a way of putting everything in perspective for all of us.

The first step in overcoming your personal difficulties in life is admitting you have a problem.

I have a problem.

There are too many stupid people.

SELF-IMPROVEMENT IS EASIER THAN I THOUGHT.

I was reminded of what Rat says in the fourth panel while watching a show where they test the knowledge of random Americans walking down the street. They asked one woman who the first person to walk on the *sun* was. She thought about it and said "Lance Armstrong."

Lord help us all.

WHERE DO YOU GET YOUR NEWS, GOAT?

I SUBSCRIBE TO THREE DIFFERENT NEWSPAPERS.

HAHA... I DON'T NEED ANY OF THAT. I JUST RELY ON MY FACEBOOK FEED FOR NEWS.

OH, YEAH? WHAT HAVE YOU LEARNED?

THAT YOUR TEDDY BEAR CAN KILL YOU, AND THE UKRAINIANS ARE SPYING ON US THROUGH OUR REFRIGERATORS.

I GUESS WE'RE BOTH INFORMED.

ALSO, EVERYONE'S GRANDFATHER HAS DIED.

Maybe that's where the woman who thought Lance Armstrong walked on the sun gets all of her information.

WISE ASS ON THE HILL →

OH, WISE ASS ON THE HILL, WHAT'S THE KEY TO PERSONAL HAPPINESS?

TO FOCUS ON THE HAPPINESS OF OTHERS.

HE'S SPOUTING GIBBERISH.

Looking back on these early Wise Ass strips, I now see I used to draw him with big pointy ears and an elongated snout. At some point I must have changed that, because he now has the ears of Danny Donkey (see below). Stuff like this sometimes happens and you don't even realize it.

WHAT ARE YOU WRITING, PIG?

A BOOK I'M CALLING 'FULL OF HIMSELF.'

ABOUT A GUY WHO'S REALLY ARROGANT?

A HIKER WHO SURVIVES BY EATING HIS OWN LEG.

WHY DO I ASK QUESTIONS?

WHY DOES THAT MAKE HIM ARROGANT?

HAHA...THIS REPUBLICAN TORCHED THIS GUY GOOD. BUT THIS DEMOCRAT FLAMED HIM RIGHT BACK.

THAT'S GREAT.

BECAUSE THE MOST IMPORTANT THING IS NOT MOVING OUR COUNTRY FORWARD, BUT DESTROYING EACH OTHER PERSONALLY.

WE FINALLY AGREE.

IF YOU NEED ME, I'LL BE CRYING IN A DARK ROOM.

I cry in the open. Right here in my comic strip.

WHAT ARE YOU READING?

THIS BOOK ON ISAAC NEWTON. IT'S AMAZING HOW MANY LAWS OF THE PHYSICAL UNIVERSE HE DISCOVERED.

I DISCOVERED ONE.

WHAT ARE YOU TALKING ABOUT?

IF YOU ARE IN A HURRY, THE PERSON IN FRONT OF YOU IN LINE WILL HAVE AN ORDER FIVE TIMES AS COMPLEX AS YOURS.

NOT QUITE NEWTONIAN.

AND WILL FUMBLE THROUGH THEIR WALLET FOR EXACT CHANGE.

In the second-to-last panel, that one man is supposed to be spraying the other man with a disinfectant. But somehow, I made it look like he was tickling him with a broom.

Speaking of which, I now post strips almost daily on Instagram. I'm at instagram.com/stephanpastis/.

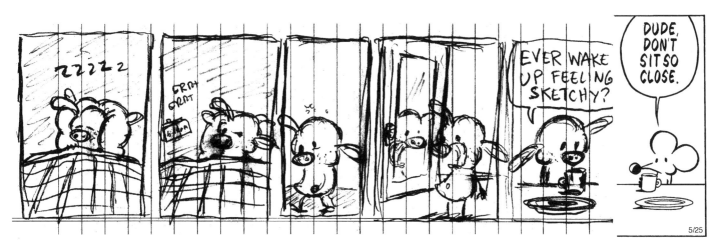

I'm not sure if I drew this one before or after the "stuck in Colombia" strips, but this was another one where I drew with pencil on a legal pad.

Here you can see I resume using the accents on résumé.

Wrong. No one wants to be a lawyer when they grow up.

5/31

The angle of this cliff somehow changes from the first panel (steep) to the second panel (flat). Perhaps there was a tectonic shift between panels.

Rat's Tip O' The Day

When people are rude to you, be above it all.

Why?

Because from up there, you can drop things on their heads.

SO THAT'S WHAT THAT EXPRESSION MEANS.

IT'S WHY IT'S SO HELPFUL.

WHAT ARE YOU READING?

THIS STORY ON THE GOVERNMENT CUTTING OFF FUNDING FOR THIS HEALTH ORGANIZATION.

WHO?

RIGHT.

WHAT?

W.H.O.

WHY?

I DON'T KNOW.

THIRD BASE!

The WHO is the World Health Organization, and they were in the news a lot in 2020.

HOW IS IT THAT YOU SEEM TO BE DOING OKAY IN THIS CRISIS?

I DO BETTER WHEN THE WORLD IS FALLING APART BECAUSE I ALWAYS EXPECT THAT TO HAPPEN AND NOW AT LEAST IT HAS.

THAT MIGHT NOT BE HEALTHY.

NOT HEALTHY IS LETTING IT SNEAK UP ON YOU.

This strip and others in this section have those hand-drawn panel lines I was doing for a while. I just liked how they looked better than the ruler-drawn lines.

This may be a good time to mention that there are also *Pearls* calendars. Below is the cover of the 2023 day-to-day calendar, which you can buy online at Amazon and other retailers.

43

During the pandemic, I was afraid to go to the barber, so one day I just shaved my head completely. I thought it looked pretty cool. My mother was aghast.

I didn't realize until right now how much this strip is basically the same as the Sunday strip that appears on the next page. Sometimes that just happens, mostly because when I submit strips to the syndicate, I often send many strips at a time, and don't necessarily notice how a Sunday strip might relate to the daily strips appearing later that week.

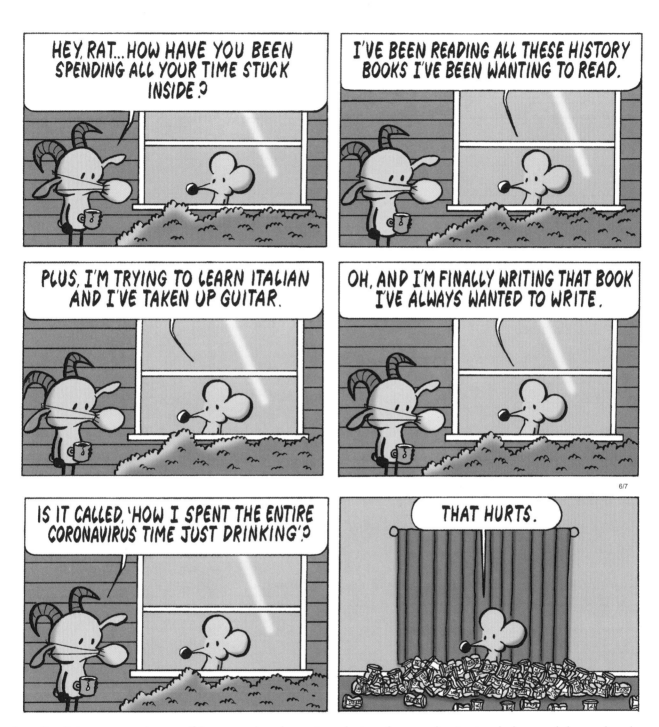

6/7

I really did try to teach myself how to play the guitar during the pandemic. I only learned three chords, but they were enough to write derogatory songs about my son, Thomas, which I sang to him at night.

I really have done this on cold days, although I do not have polka-dot underwear. I would include a photo of my actual underwear here, but my book editor, Lucas Wetzel, tells me that's not necessary.

Believe it or not, this is another strip that the syndicate would have nixed just a few years back. The word "sucked" was totally off-limits. Now, it's more or less allowed.

DUDE, IT'S NOON... WHY ARE YOU STILL IN BED?

BECAUSE NOTHING THAT WILL HAPPEN TODAY WILL BE BETTER THAN THE WARMTH AND COMFORT THAT I HAVE HERE.

YOU MAY HAVE SOLVED LIFE.

This strip is a repeat. It ran on this day because my syndicate would not let me run the strip I had originally submitted, which was a pun on the name of the town Boise, Idaho. I think they thought that too many newspapers would find it offensive. But as this is a book, not a newspaper, you can judge for yourself:

Okay, boys, me got plan catch da zeeba. Me dress as woomun of night. Zeeba let me een house.

You reely tink you can pass as woomun?

Of course me can. You is wait here.

Boys, see... I da ho!

OFFENSIVE ON MANY LEVELS.

BOISE LOVES ME.

THIS POLITICIAN SEEMS TO LIE EVERY TIME HE TALKS.

SOUNDS LIKE HE NEEDS A DEFIBRILLATOR.

WHY A DEFIBRILLATOR?

KNOCKS THE FIB RIGHT OUT OF YOU.

NOT WHAT THAT IS.

THEY USE MORE VOLTS FOR POLITICIANS.

47

I am constantly forgetting people's names. It becomes apparent when I'm at a party and have to introduce my wife to someone I've known for years. And boom, I forget my wife's name.

Small note regarding my last comment: That was a joke. My wife's name is Staci. And I remember it by writing it on the back of my hand.

I went the opposite direction as my comic incarnation by totally shaving my head.

Looking at this strip, I can clearly see the influence that Bugs Bunny cartoons used to have on me. Daffy Duck and Bugs would always hold up signs like this.

This really did happen. I was walking outside during the early days of the pandemic and a woman was coming the other way down the sidewalk. I guess she thought I was too near her on the sidewalk, so she pointed at me and shouted, "Six feet please!"

This is me in front of the Colosseum. (Along with my mother. Who I took there for her 80th birthday. Oh, sorry, Mom—*60th* birthday.)

I believe none other than Mark Hamill himself liked this strip on Twitter. You can find me on Twitter at https://twitter.com/stephanpastis.

Not quite sure where that mallet came from, given that you can see the entire pod and there's no mallet anywhere. We'll just call it comic strip magic.

I tried to read a book on quantum physics. The only words I understood in the entire book were "Introduction" and "The End."

Speaking of physics, how Pig's tie remains on his body is anyone's guess. Perhaps he glues it to his chest.

A MOM STORY
by Rat

MOM, I'VE COME OVER HERE TODAY TO ASK YOU WHY YOU DIDN'T PAY MORE ATTENTION TO ME WHEN I WAS LITTLE.

WELL, WHEN I HAD YOU I WAS SO YOUNG.

AND I WANTED TO DO SO MANY THINGS WITH MY LIFE AND I COULDN'T DO SOME OF THOSE THINGS AFTER I HAD YOU.

AND I THINK I STUPIDLY FELT KIND OF RESENTFUL.

WAIT A MINUTE.

WHAT?

SO IN ADDITION TO BEING A MOM, YOU WERE ALSO A REGULAR PERSON WITH REGULAR PERSON FEELINGS?

6/28

Yes.

AND THAT'S WHEN HIS STUNNED, LITTLE BRAIN EXPLODED.

MOMS ARE WHAT NOW?

Look at how the shape of that tree changes in every panel. It's a miracle of nature.

54

As things seemed to get darker and darker in 2020, I kept trying to make Pig happier and happier. Someone had to balance all that out.

I based this in part on an actual kid I heard about. During his online classes, he replaced himself with a graphic that said his internet connection was temporarily out and then went and did other things with his day.

The "barbaric act" here is in reference to the killing of George Floyd in Minneapolis, Minnesota, in May 2020.

This, too, was in reference to the event mentioned above. It really did seem in the spring of 2020 that the world was falling apart.

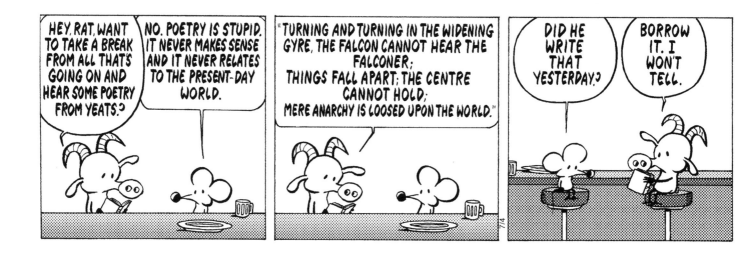

THE FEW GOOD THINGS IN THE BADNESS THAT IS NOW

FEWER SOCIAL GATHERINGS.

YAY FOR INTROVERTS.

NO MORE NEED TO MAKE EXCUSES FOR NOT GOING TO THOSE SOCIAL GATHERINGS.

GEE, I SPRAINED MY TOE MAKING ORANGE JUICE SO I CAN'T—WAIT—THE STAY-AT-HOME ORDER! THE STAY-AT-HOME ORDER!

COLLEGE-AGE KIDS BACK HOME.

WANNA PLAY?

NOPE.

NO MORE CARING HOW I LOOK.

ME SASQUATCH!

7/5

SITTING AROUND ALL DAY DRINKING BEER NOW PERFECTLY ACCEPTABLE.

THIS IS LIVING.

WELL, ALMOST.

YOU GONNA DO THIS ALL DAY?

SWEETIE, PLEASE. IT'S THINKY TIME.

CARTOONIST AT WORK

There's a fine line between writing and laziness. From an outsider's perspective, I'm sure they look identical. Or at least that's what I tell my wife.

I love simple strips like this the most. But they're generally the hardest to write.

Admit it—you just tried it. Oh, the power of cartoons.

Surely, someone else has thought of this.

The string from Goat's tea bag is not present in the first panel but suddenly appears in the next two panels. Give yourself five *Pearls* points if you noticed that. (Note: *Pearls* points are redeemable from Andrews McMeel Syndication for large cash payouts.)

59

I'M SO BORED OF THIS WHOLE COVID THING, STEPH.

WELL, HERE'S SOMETHING FUN, PIG. YOUR SPEECH BALLOON IS AN ACTUAL BALLOON. JUST GRAB THE TAIL.

IT **IS** FUN! I CAN SEE THE WHOLE COMICS PAGE FROM HERE!

YEAH. JUST MAKE SURE YOU DON'T STOP TALK-ING OR YOU'LL HAVE NO—

BALLOON.

Apologies to my ever-patient friend, Jeff Keane. Please do not sue.

"Mommy, God dropped a pig on Dolly!"

I could see God really doing this to one of the *Family Circus* kids. Just for sport.

I'm going places!

AWW... THAT'S A GREAT ATTITUDE, PIG. ESPECIALLY THESE DAYS.

First, the Poorhouse.

NEVER MIND.

Then, debtor's prison.

Note from the Legal Department of Andrews McMeel Syndication: *In the comment below the July 11, 2020, strip, Mr. Pastis made a claim regarding* Pearls *points being redeemable for cash. This is not true and should not be relied upon.*

WHAZAM

KABLOOEY

TAXES WILL NOT MAGICALLY DO THEMSELVES.

WHAT ARE YOU TWO DOING?

KEEPING AN EYE ON LIFE. WE'RE CERTAIN IT HAS SOME TERRIBLE SURPRISE IN STORE FOR US, SO WE'RE HIDING AND STAYING ALERT.

WHAT AN AWFUL WAY TO GO THROUGH LIFE. I PREFER TO ENJOY EACH AND EVERY DAY.

HE'S LOST IT.

Amateurs hide behind couches. Pros hide in closets.

Fun Fact: I cannot fix anything. So when something breaks, I contact my wife and tell her to save me because the world is ending. It's that kind of melodramatic whining that makes me so attractive as a spouse.

Seriously, subscribe to a local newspaper. Because when they go away, you'll really miss them. And if they go away, my strip goes away. And you would really, really, really, really, really, really, really miss me.

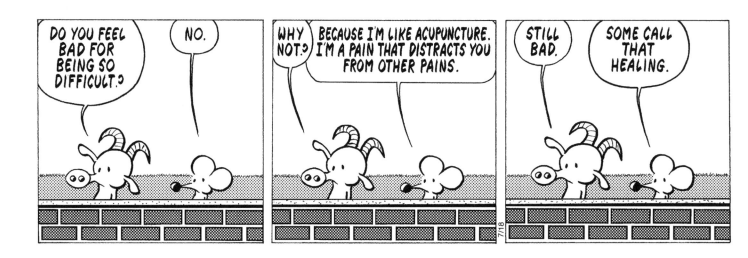

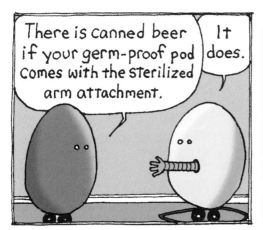

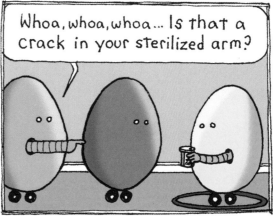

The thing I will remember the most from the early days of the pandemic is wearing dishwashing gloves to the grocery store. I looked beautiful.

Panel 2: AWW...THAT MAKES ME FEEL BETTER.

Panel 1 sign: TOMORROW IS ANOTHER DAY.

Panel 2 sign: TOMORROW IS ANOTHER DAY.

Panel 3 sign: AND IT MIGHT BE WORSE THAN THIS ONE.

Panel 4: MY BETTERNESS IS FEELING LESS BETTERY.

Panel 4 sign: JUST TRYING TO BE REALISTIC HERE.

Hey, kids—"bettery" is not yet a word. But if you include it in all your homework assignments, it will become one. And be sure to give me credit. Unless it causes you to fail, in which case, blame your parents.

Panel 1: The key to happiness is to worry less.

Panel 2: THAT'S GREAT, PIG. HOW DO YOU RECOMMEND DOING THAT?

Panel 3: Have no problems in your life.

Panel 4: I JUST MASTERED EXISTENCE.

Panel 1: DO YOU THINK LIFE IS ABSURD? / I THINK IT'S MORE WONDERFUL THAN ABSURD.

Panel 2: DID YOU KNOW THERE IS AN ACCOUNTING HALL OF FAME?

Panel 3: OKAY, MAYBE MORE ABSURD. / DO YOU THINK THE BUILDING IS A GIANT GREEN VISOR?

There really is an Accounting Hall of Fame and it is located in Columbus, Ohio. Imagine the excitement.

I mention bonbons a lot in the strip. Which is strange because I don't think I've ever had a bonbon.

For all my talk of drinking in the strip, I would never drink before writing. I won't even take an aspirin. I'm really paranoid about disturbing whatever chemical balance is necessary to write.

I have it on good authority that the person who drew this strip took the toilet paper image from the second panel and lazily cut-and-pasted it into the next three panels. Feel free to seek a refund for this portion of the book.

You may be wondering, given that there is no headboard, what it is that Pig's pillow is propped up against. I am wondering that as well.

I didn't understand one thing that happened in either of those movies. So either Christopher Nolan makes indecipherable movies or I am much dumber than the general population.

My son, Thomas, just read the comment under that last strip and said, "The latter." Thomas is not half as funny as he thinks he is.

My son, Thomas, just read the comment under that last strip and said, "Look who's talking." Now I'm thinking of taking his food away.

This was one of the most popular strips of the year.

I call Twitter "the sad place" because it always seems to depress me. And yet I still go on there all the time.

For the last two years (basically since the start of the pandemic), I've read almost nothing but travel guidebooks. I think it's because when you can't travel, it's at least nice to fantasize about it.

MY DAILY WORRIES BROKEN DOWN BY PERCENTAGES:

40% - WORRIES ABOUT THINGS THAT HAVE HAPPENED.
30% - WORRIES ABOUT THINGS THAT WILL HAPPEN.
29% - WORRIES ABOUT THINGS THAT MAY HAPPEN.

1% - NOT WORRYING AND THEREBY WORRYING THAT I'M LETTING MY GUARD DOWN.

FUN DAY.

I WORRIED YOU'D SAY THAT.

I think I've gotten much better about worrying less. Though I'm worried that could change.

HEY, RAT, WHAT DO YOU HAVE THERE?

WINE. I SPLURGED LIKE A RICH PERSON AND BOUGHT A $1,000 BOTTLE OF CABERNET, WHICH I'M ABOUT TO TRY.

DRINK DRINK DRINK

WELL, WHAT'S IT TASTE LIKE?

WINE.

EVER FEEL LIKE ALL OF LIFE IS ONE BIG HOAX?

YES! AND I'M NEVER IN ON IT!

Next month I'm going to my first-ever, super-sophisticated wine tasting in Napa Valley, CA. Apparently, you're not supposed to actually drink the wine, but instead, spit it into a "spit bucket." The thing I'm looking forward to the most is making a loud sound when I do it.

DID YOU SEE THESE NEW GUIDELINES FROM THE CENTERS FOR DISEASE CONTROL?

OH, GREAT... HERE WE ALL ARE AGAINST THIS DISEASE CONTROLLING OUR LIVES AND THESE GUYS ARE FOR IT?

I THINK I'VE LOST YOU.

PLEASE DON'T TELL ME MY TAXES PAY FOR THAT.

I recently did an interview with the NPR station in Little Rock, Arkansas, where the interviewer told me this was his favorite strip of the year. That's just a long way of saying I'm so important I'm interviewed by NPR stations.

The truth is that I was more productive during the lockdown phase of the pandemic than at any other point of my life. In addition to the strip, I wrote two graphic novels (*Trubble Town*, Volumes 1 and 2) and a new chapter book called *Looking Up*.

You have to admit this is a great idea.

During most of the pandemic, I took almost the same 3-mile walk every day. And while I walked, I tried to think up ideas for the strip. There's something about walking that really helps you think creatively.

I recently read the travel guidebook for Morocco. And as soon as these Covid travel restrictions are lifted, I'm gonna go.

Somehow Rat's dialogue in the first panel seems vaguely inappropriate. I shall make no further comment.

I believe I got my first vaccine dose in April 2021. There were other people ahead of me in line, so I just pushed them out of the way. I believe three of them were elderly.

Oddly, masks somehow became a big political issue. So this was a pretty popular strip.

Sometimes I go out with people I know, and without telling me, they'll post photos of it on social media. That always strikes me as kind of odd.

This was a strategy I started employing during the pandemic. Things just got too depressing.

I care so little about cars that when someone asks me what I drive, it takes me a minute to remember. (Toyota Avalon, my wife just said.)

The amazing thing is that the illusionist David Blaine actually achieved this, floating almost 25,000 feet into the sky. Google "David Blaine balloons" to see it.

The reason my characters speak behind a wall is that Charlie Brown and Linus used to do it in *Peanuts*. I stole almost all of my backgrounds from Charles Schulz and actually got to meet him and tell him that. He told me that he in turn had stolen *his* backgrounds from Percy Crosby, the creator of *Skippy*.

This is true.

OH, GREAT WISE ASS, WHAT IS THE KEY TO ENDING THIS VIRUS?

STAYING SIX FEET AWAY FROM EACH OTHER.

BOOT

SOMETIMES YOU HAVE TO LEAD BY EXAMPLE.

I see Wise Ass still has those pointy ears here, which is making me very curious as to when I changed his look. I assume it will occur at some point during the strips in this book.

HEY, PIG, WHAT ARE YOU UP TO THIS QUARANTINE WEEKEND?

A WHOLE LOT OF S AND M.

YOU? REALLY?

YEAH. YOU NEVER SIT AND MOPE?

PERHAPS WE SHOULD DEFINE OUR TERMS.

EVERYONE'S DOING IT.

At some point in the summer of 2020, I got tired of sitting and moping, so I got in a rental car and drove all over Missouri, Kansas, Nebraska, South Dakota, North Dakota, Minnesota, and Iowa. I brought along the former president of my syndicate, John Glynn, who caught a flight home after I accidentally drove the car into oncoming highway traffic. Here he is enjoying the Sod House Museum that I made him visit on a 100-degree day.

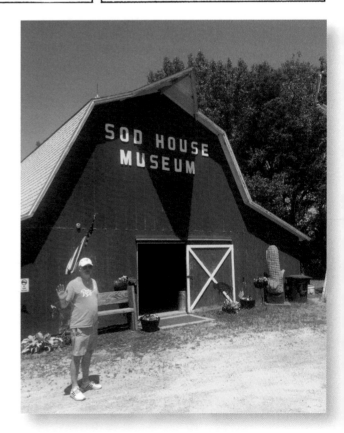

8/30

Wise Ass is my most popular new character. I can say that with some confidence as he is also my *only* new character.

HAPPY BIRTHDAY, GOAT.

MY BIRTHDAY'S NOT FOR SIX MONTHS.

YES, BUT I CAN NEVER REMEMBER ANYONE'S BIRTHDAY, SO I SAY IT WHEN I THINK OF IT AND YOUR JOB IS TO REMEMBER IT SIX MONTHS FROM NOW.

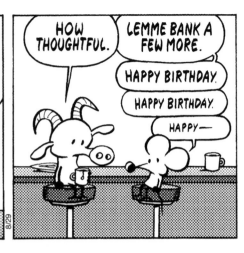

HOW THOUGHTFUL.

LEMME BANK A FEW MORE.

HAPPY BIRTHDAY.

HAPPY BIRTHDAY.

HAPPY—

I'VE DECIDED THAT FROM NOW ON, I'M GONNA BE UPBEAT AT THE START OF EACH NEW WEEK AND ONLY WORRY ABOUT THE THINGS I CAN CONTROL. HOW 'BOUT YOU?

I'M MAKING PLANS TO FIGHT TO THE DEATH FOR THE FEW RESOURCES WE'LL SOON HAVE LEFT.

SOME GUYS YOU SHOULD AVOID ON MONDAYS.

DO PEOPLE STILL USE THESE?

My roommate in college once said he liked hanging around me because he knew that if the apocalypse happened and there was only one can of beans left, he could beat me up and take it.

DID YOU JUST DOUBLE PARK?

YEAH.

WHAT IF OTHER PEOPLE DID THAT TO YOU?

I'D BE ANGRY.

SO?

SO FOR THE WORLD TO FUNCTION SMOOTHLY, EVERYONE NEEDS TO ACT A LOT BETTER THAN I DO.

NOT HOW THE WORLD WORKS.

AND THAT'S WHAT MAKES LIFE SO HARD.

Poor, dumb Pig might actually be the smartest character in the strip.

Social media "doom spirals" became quite the thing in 2020. I sometimes found myself leaving my phone in the car at night, just so I wouldn't look at it.

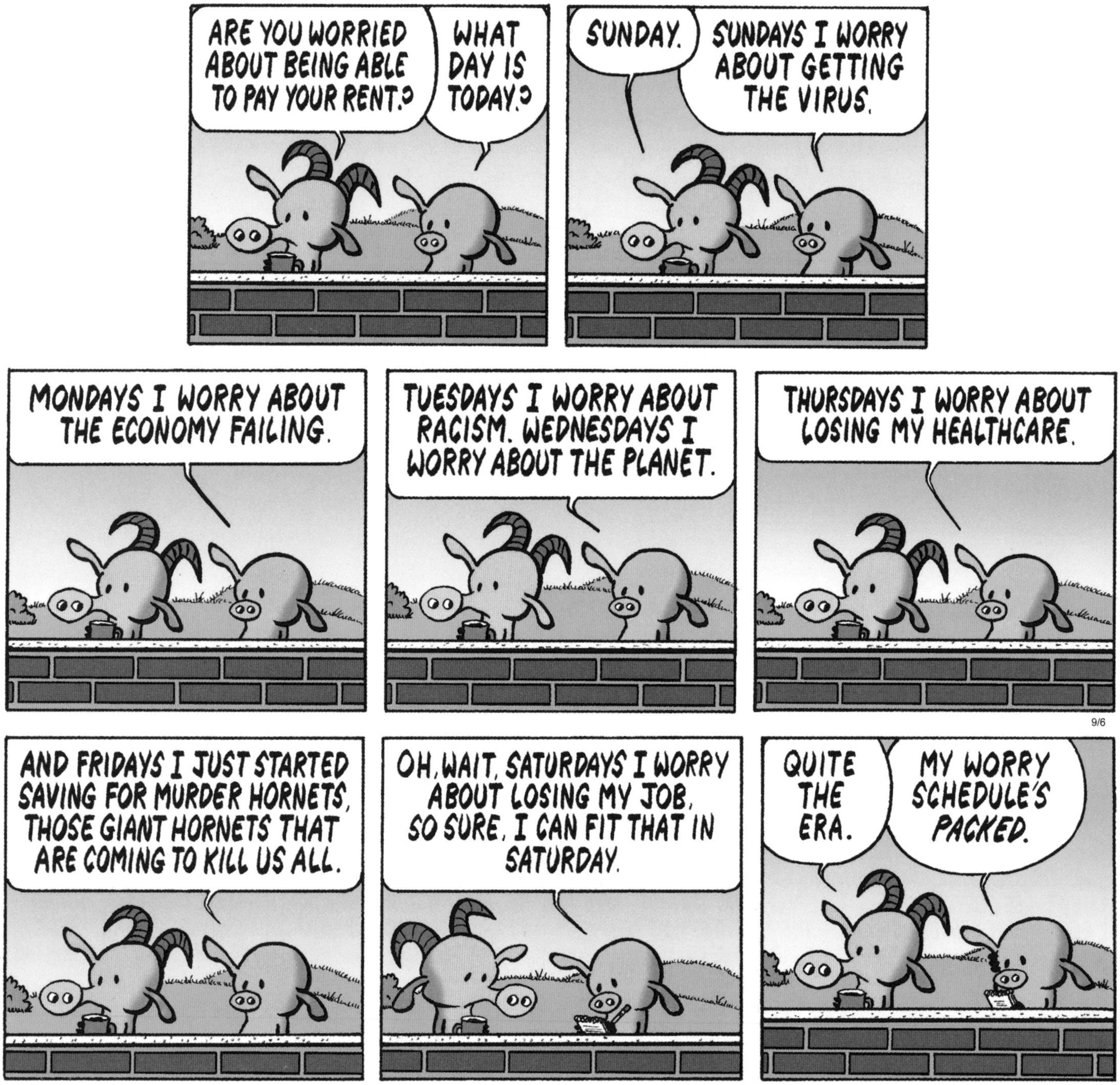
ARE YOU WORRIED ABOUT BEING ABLE TO PAY YOUR RENT?
WHAT DAY IS TODAY?
SUNDAY.
SUNDAYS I WORRY ABOUT GETTING THE VIRUS.
MONDAYS I WORRY ABOUT THE ECONOMY FAILING.
TUESDAYS I WORRY ABOUT RACISM. WEDNESDAYS I WORRY ABOUT THE PLANET.
THURSDAYS I WORRY ABOUT LOSING MY HEALTHCARE.
9/6
AND FRIDAYS I JUST STARTED SAVING FOR MURDER HORNETS, THOSE GIANT HORNETS THAT ARE COMING TO KILL US ALL.
OH, WAIT, SATURDAYS I WORRY ABOUT LOSING MY JOB, SO SURE, I CAN FIT THAT IN SATURDAY.
QUITE THE ERA.
MY WORRY SCHEDULE'S *PACKED*.

There are many people who could benefit from this advice. But not me. I'm great as is.

My wife read the comment I made under the last strip and asked for space to list all the things that are wrong with me. I asked how much space she needed, and she said, "The rest of the book." I didn't find that funny.

While I've never had an out-of-body experience, I once dreamt that I had died. It was followed by complete and total silence, like I was suddenly in a vacuum chamber. Then I began to hear the loudest, shrillest sound I'd ever heard. It was so piercing that I thought it was going to damage my hearing, and so I somehow shook myself awake. It was one of the strangest experiences of my life.

That's supposed to be a wig in the second panel. It is not an oversized lima bean. Thank God I have books to explain these things.

I intentionally ran this strip on a Wednesday because Friday was two days away and there would be time for Rat to save money. It's little details like that which make *Pearls* the masterpiece of comic art that it is.

I have this thought every time I see a guy drive past me in a truck that's been jacked up really high. And my apologies to anyone reading this who has a truck that's jacked up really high.

I'll tell you right now—The only reason I did this strip was to see if I could get away with putting "GREAT BOOB" in the comic strip. Turns out that I could.

Panel 1: WHAT ARE YOU READING, PIG? / A HORROR NOVEL ABOUT THIS GUY NAMED JOE WHO'S MURDERED BY HIS WIFE AND CHOPPED UP INTO LITTLE PIECES.

Panel 2: SOUNDS TERRIFYING. / YEAH...IT'S GIVING ME NIGHTMARES.

Panel 3: CUP O' JOE?

Panel 4: HARD TO EXPLAIN. / MAYBE HE SHOULD SWITCH TO DECAF.

Panel 1: I THINK THE KEY TO SURVIVING TIMES LIKE THESE IS TO EACH HAVE A LITTLE STAIRWAY TO THE STARS THAT YOU CAN CLIMB TO GET AWAY.

Panel 2: I THINK THE KEY IS TO NOT UTTER USELESS GIBBERISH.

Panel 3: LET'S SEE WHOSE WAY'S BETTER.

Panel 4: I SHOULD BE LESS CYNICAL.

The truth is that if you tried to climb to the stars, you'd run out of oxygen at 26,000 feet and die. But other than that, it's a wonderful idea.

Panel 1: WHAT ARE YOU DOING WITH YOUR CALENDAR? / TOSSING IT. I'VE DECIDED THAT 2020 NEVER EXISTED. / TOSS

Panel 2: NONE OF THE THINGS THAT HAPPENED HAPPENED. NONE OF US GOT OLDER. NONE OF US MISSED ANYTHING.

Panel 3: DIDN'T KNOW IT WAS THAT EASY. / DID I STILL DRINK ALL THAT GIN?

Gin and tonic is my go-to drink whenever I go to bars. Not because I like them, but because it's the only drink I can remember.

I really do think we're now being led by a generation of politicians who like power for the sake of power. Many could do the right thing, but choose instead to protect their political career.

This is a wonderful idea. I would do it, but I'd lose half the year apologizing.

For the cover of the last treasury (*Pearls Awaits the Tide*), I had the photographer bury me up to my neck at the beach. I didn't realize that the weight of the sand puts so much pressure on your chest that it's a bit difficult to breath. It is not for the claustrophobic.

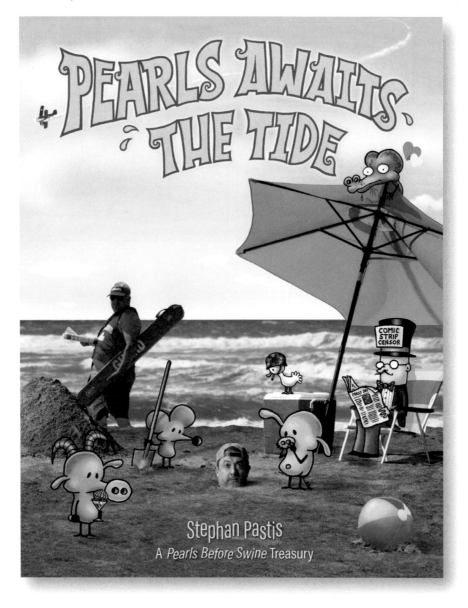

This happens every time I make a joke about the assassination of Lincoln. Maybe in 2,000 years it will be possible to tell those jokes.

Sometimes when I speak at grade schools for my *Timmy Failure* books, a kid will ask me how much money I make. I always say, "More than you, you little snot. Now shut your mouth."

Panel 1:
HEY, WE JUST GOT A LETTER FROM 'THE POWERS THAT BE IN THE UNIVERSE.'
LET'S SEE IT.

Panel 2:
Dear Everyone,
As you know, we try to balance every year with both good and bad.

Panel 3:
But this year...
Oopsie Doopsie!

Panel 4:
THAT'S ALMOST AN APOLOGY.
I DON'T LIKE THEIR ATTITUDE.

Regarding that last comment, I do not actually tell elementary school children to shut their mouths. I do, however, call them "little snots." And sometimes I throw in profanity.

 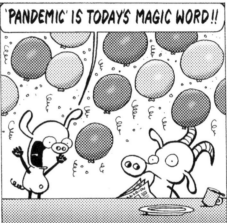 

Panel 1:
HEY, GOAT, WHAT'S GOING ON?
OH, JUST READING SOME STORIES ABOUT THE PANDEMIC.

Panel 2:
'PANDEMIC' IS TODAY'S MAGIC WORD!!

Panel 3:
JUST TRYING TO TURN A NEGATIVE INTO A POSITIVE.

For a while, I had to stop reading the *New York Times* in the morning because they always published the number of people who had died from Covid that day (and as of the writing of these comments in June 2022, they still do). It was just too grim.

Panel 1:
WELL, GUESS WHO'S NOW AN EXPERT ON GOTHIC ARCHITECTURE!
WHAT MADE YOU WANT TO LEARN ABOUT BORING ARCHITECTURE?

Panel 2:
'CAUSE SOMEONE TOLD ME ABOUT THIS BIG BUTTOCK FLYING AROUND IN THE SKY! AND I SAID, 'A BIG FLYING BUTT IN THE SKY? NOW *THAT'S* SOMETHING I GOTTA LEARN ABOUT!'

Panel 3:
THEY'RE CALLED 'FLYING BUTTRESSES.' NOT 'FLYING BUTTOCKS.'

Panel 4:
ARCHITECTURE'S BORING AGAIN.

If you're wondering why there are five guests but only four cups, it's because
Mr. Clowney is a recovering alcoholic and cannot partake.

For me, the best part of living in this age is the ability to look up anything I'm curious about. And while I'd like to say my searches are intellectual and scholarly, usually it's "videos of fat guy falling."

Wise Ass update: Still has pointy ears.

As much as I talk about beer in the strip, the truth is I don't know very much about it. So I recently bought a book called *Beer for Dummies* so that when bartenders ask me what kind of beer I like, I can stop just saying, "The cold kind."

In the early years of the strip, the grass backgrounds in *Pearls* always used to be straight lines. But now they're almost always hilly. I'm guessing you found that so fascinating you just fell over in your chair.

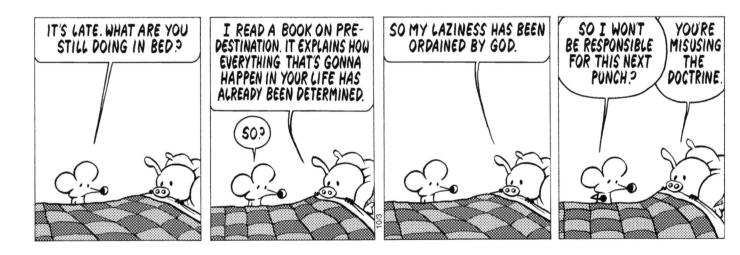

"Never Try to Better Yourself" is the title of my upcoming talk at an elementary school. Though I'm thinking about adding "You Little Snot" at the end.

97

Once again, Pig was my go-to character to lighten the mood during a pretty dark time.

IT HATH OCCURRED! This was apparently the moment that I changed the look of the Wise Ass's ears. I'd like to say it was intentional, but really, I just screwed up.

I believe at least a couple newspapers refused to run this. The word "turd" is apparently too offensive and can only be used in books.

Turd turd turd turd turd turd turd turd turd turd turd turd turd turd turd turd turd turd turd turd turd turd turd turd turd turd turd turd turd turd turd turd turd turd turd turd turd turd turd turd turd turd turd turd turd turd turd turd turd turd turd turd turd turd turd turd turd turd turd turd turd turd turd turd turd turd turd turd turd turd turd turd turd.

HI, GUYS, THANKS FOR JOINING THE ZOOM CALL.

AS YOU KNOW, THIS OFFICE WILL REMAIN CLOSED FOR THE FORESEE-ABLE FUTURE, SO WE'LL KEEP DOING THESE EMPLOYEE MEETINGS ONLINE.

AND AGAIN, WE KNOW THESE ARE DIFFICULT TIMES...

...AND THAT YOU'RE ALL AT HOME, AND MANY OF YOU DON'T HAVE HOME OFFICES.

SO WE WANT TO TRY TO KEEP THESE MEETINGS AS CASUAL AS POSSIBLE.

BUT, RAT, I THINK WHATEVER YOU'RE DOING IS PUSHING IT.

10/11

IT'S CALLED A BEER BELLY TOWER.

THESE CALLS ARE RAPIDLY DEVOLVING.

MY HOUSE, MY RULES, PEOPLE.

When we were all trapped at home during the pandemic, me and two of my friends started randomly setting up Zoom calls with former classmates from high school who we hadn't seen in 35 years. Which seems like a good idea until you actually do it, and afterward say to yourself, "I really didn't miss that guy."

Strip 1, Panel 1:
WHAT ARE YOU WRITING, PIG?

I ALWAYS LIKE TO PUT TOGETHER A DETAILED PLAN FOR THE UPCOMING WEEK. IT MAKES ME A LOT MORE PRODUCTIVE.

Panel 2:
THAT SOUNDS REALLY SMART. CAN I SEE IT?

SURE.

Panel 3:
Monday: Get through today.
Tuesday: Get through today.
Wednesday: Get through today.
Thursday: Get through today.
Friday: Get through today.
Saturday: Get through today.
Sunday: Get through today.

Panel 4:
THE NEXT FORTY YEARS LOOKS MUCH THE SAME.

Strip 2, Panel 1:
HI, PIG, WHAT'S UP?

I'VE DECIDED TO GO DOOR-TO-DOOR HUGGING PEOPLE. BECAUSE I THINK OUR ONLY WAY OUT OF THESE DIFFICULT DAYS IS TO HUG OUR WAY OUT.

Panel 2:
WE CAN'T HUG ANYMORE. IT'LL JUST SPREAD THE VIRUS.

Panel 3:
THESE ARE MERCILESS TIMES.

I hugged people anyway, but then made sure they were safe by brushing the germs off of them.

Strip 3, Panel 1:
PIG SEEMS A LOT HAPPIER LATELY.

YEAH, HE NO LONGER LETS THE NEWS GET HIM DOWN.

Panel 2:
WISH I COULD DO THAT. WHAT'S HIS SECRET?

HE SHUTS HIS EYES AND COVERS HIS EARS.

Panel 3:
LALALALALA

Panel 4:
THAT'S ONE WAY.

LIFE IS GREAT!

You may be wondering what happened to the background in those first two panels. I am also.

This really is solid advice. Another piece of solid advice is don't forget the backgrounds in your comic strip.

I believe Reed now uses this as his Twitter profile photo. And I don't blame him. It's very flattering.
(Sidenote: That's my Timmy Failure character on the wall.)

People seemed to really like this strip. Another case of Pig offering a ray of hope in tough times.

This strip arose from phone conversations I had with my mom during the pandemic. I would casually ask, "What's new?" and she'd say, "Honey, nothing is new. I do the same thing every day." Then she'd tell me to "Shut the f&$# up."

Note regarding the last comment: I may have taken some artistic license with that quote by my mother. As a general rule, she does not drop many f-bombs.

This strip was published in October 2020, which was around the time I took the trip mentioned in the Introduction. One of the highlights of the trip was Monument Valley, Arizona. Find me if you can.

Dear World,
You've done lots to try and bring me down this year.

But I'm still standing.

IN YOUR FACE, WORLD.

SOMETIMES YOU GOTTA LET THE WORLD KNOW WHO'S BOSS.

10/23

Speaking of still standing, the other highlight of the trip was White Sands National Park in New Mexico, where I got this cool shot of me atop one of the dunes. If you've never been there, you really should go. It's incredible.

HEY, RAT, HOW COME YOU'RE NOT AT THE CAFE TODAY?

THE WORLD'S FALLING APART, SO I'M TAKING OFF.

10/24

AND GOING WHERE?
TO LIVE IN A BIG FLUFFY CLOUD.

YOU KNOW A CLOUD IS NOT EXACTLY—

AAAHHHH
WHUMP!

SOLID.
DOES EVERYWHERE SUCK NOW?

My wife's aunt Kathy made a costume of Larry that I recently wore for Halloween. I looked quite dashing.

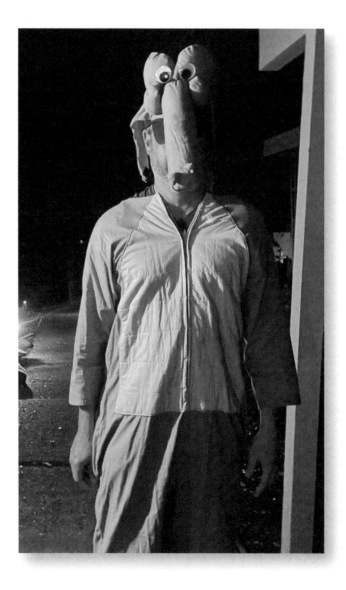

My book editor, Lucas Wetzel, just informed me that running three photos in a row has really screwed up the layout of this book. These things happen.

My son, Thomas, is gluten intolerant. So whenever he opens up a gluten-free package, I make this joke. He never laughs. Which I guess makes him dad intolerant too.

I think I've done election-related strips around the time of each presidential election, such as here, in the fall of 2020, when Joe Biden was running against the orange guy.

Looking back at it, I think something's off about this particular strip. It's just a bit too preachy or jingoistic.

Roughly 63 percent of Americans cannot name their Representative in Congress. And 20 percent don't even know that Congress is a branch of our government. Though a whopping 98 percent find me handsome.

Speaking of islands, I'll be making my first post-pandemic trip out of the country next month when I head to Puerto Rico.

Fact check regarding that last comment: I've just been informed that Puerto Rico is actually a part of our country. At least I can name our four branches of government.

Becoming a Better Writer

Compelling fiction writing is often based on personal experience.

Today I stayed in my house. Later I went to bed.

THIS IS A BAD TIME FOR WRITERS.

Fact-check regarding that last fact-check: I've just been informed there are only three branches of government.

AS THERE IS NOW NO DIFFERENCE BETWEEN ANY OF THE DAYS, I AM ELIMINATING THE WORDS 'MONDAY,' 'TUESDAY,' 'WEDNESDAY,' 'THURSDAY,' 'FRIDAY,' 'SATURDAY,' AND 'SUNDAY.'

INSTEAD, WE WILL NOW JUST CALL EVERY DAY 'DAYDAY.'

FOR EXAMPLE, "WHAT ARE YOU DOING NEXT DAYDAY?" ..."OH, THE THING I DID LAST DAYDAY."

I HATE DAYDAYS.

After this strip ran, I got a great note from *Garfield* creator Jim Davis who said, "Read the first frame this morning and thought, 'Now there's a career-ending concept for Garfield.' Then I nearly fell off my chair when I saw the punch line." It led to a great Zoom call where we talked about comics, the pandemic, and other things. He's an incredibly nice person.

The man spotted his suit jacket hanging from the cliff.

So he grabbed the jacket and put it on.

Leaving only the hanger. **THE END.**

CLIFF HANGER ENDING.

YOUR CAREER NEEDS AN ENDING ENDING.

11/8

I was in Vietnam a few years ago and had an opportunity to crawl into the tunnels used by the North Vietnamese during the Vietnam War. But they are incredibly tight and narrow, and so I fled crying.

Note regarding that last comment: I am tough and have never once cried.

Note regarding that last comment about the last comment: My wife, Staci, who is almost never helpful in these books, would like you to know that I cried the night Princess Diana died.

If you have any idea how my characters get up onto these very high stools, please let me know.

Even just saying the phrase "sexual orientation" on the comics page can be an iffy proposition. Some editors want no mention of sex at all. But I am fearless and defy them.

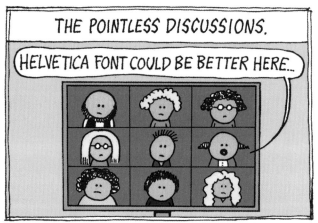

Regarding that last comment about me being fearless: My wife, Staci, who is once again being unhelpful, would like you to know that one time at a lake a swan charged me and I ran away screaming like a toddler.

During my USO visit to Iraq during the war, I got to wear an army helmet for the very first time. And so I taped a note to it:

Note to those of you who outlive me: I would like the title "Father of Wit" chiseled upon my headstone. Spare no expense.

I'll be honest—I don't even know what a cannoli is. All I know is that it's part of a very famous line from *The Godfather*: "Leave the gun. Take the cannoli."

I have to say, if there was any good aspect of the pandemic, it was getting out of all social events. It was a built-in excuse to not have to go anywhere.

Other than that one pointy little boob, you'd have no way of knowing that woman I drew is supposed to be a woman. It could just as easily be a man with a mullet and a chest tumor.

I don't really have any specific comment for this strip. So this might be as good a time as any to tell you that in my bedroom I keep a baby doll camouflaged as a houseplant.

Rat always looks so odd when he smiles. It's never comforting.

MENTAL HEALTH QUIZ

Please answer the following questions about how you currently feel:

Stressed? _____
Lonely? _____
Disgusted? _____

Sad? _____
Scared? _____
Annoyed? _____

Anxious? _____
Tired? _____
Depressed? _____

Irritable? _____
Frustrated? _____
Mad? _____

IT'S NICE WHEN ONE ANSWER FITS ALL.

YOU TORE THROUGH THE PAPER.

I think I might actually have torn through the paper while drawing that second-to-last panel.

11/29

122

We have a leaf blower at our house. My wife, Staci, would like you to know that I have never once used it.

Here's all I know about writing poetry: Write something no one else understands and one day people will call you a genius.

If I were to do a book of only 2020 strips, I think the image of Pig in the third panel would be the cover.

Panel 1: WHAT CAN I GET YOU? / GIMME A LAGER.

Panel 3: MAY A REDWOOD CRUSH YOUR UNFUNNY HEAD.

All beers are either a lager or an ale or a hybrid of the two. You may not find that interesting, but as I said earlier, I'm currently reading a book about beer and have no one else to tell that to.

Panel 1: WORKING AT HOME DURING THE PANDEMIC HAS REALLY CHANGED HOW I SEE MY WORKDAY.

Panel 2: YEAH, YOU MEAN HOW YOU DON'T NEED TO GO INTO AN OFFICE AND CAN DO MOST STUFF FROM HOME?

Panel 3: HOW GIVEN A FULLY STOCKED KITCHEN, I WILL VISIT IT EVERY EIGHT MINUTES.

Panel 4: RIGHT. / I'M THINKING ABOUT MOVING MY DESK INTO THE PANTRY.

I have removed all snack items from my studio, because I would literally eat everything in one afternoon.

Panel 1: SOON, EVERYTHING WE'RE GOING THROUGH WILL BE OVER. / I SURE HOPE SO. I'M SO TIRED OF THIS VIRUS.

Panel 2: OH, I MEANT THE WORLD ENDING. MOST LIKELY BY NUCLEAR WAR.

Panel 3: NEVER MIND. / I THOUGHT YOU SOUNDED A BIT TOO CHEERY.

I love these uplifting strips the most.

Elly Elephant was lonely.

So she swiped right on a dating app and met her date for coffee.

Why'd you want to meet for coffee instead of my house tonight for dinner?

Well, dinner implies a little too much. And your house, well, that's just nuts.

How is this cafe better?

Well, if things got unpleasant, there are people around, and I could scream.

12/6

I just wanted to show you my house. It's 8,000 square feet. I guess that isn't surprising given my salary and the car I drove up in. Money says everything about a guy.

AHHHHHHHHHHH

Elly Elephant decided loneliness was a wonderful thing.

The café here is named for the owner of the Calistoga Roastery in Calistoga, California, where I drew the strip for many years.

I was bored recently and started messaging a food delivery app telling them I was on the roof of my two-story house because my angry wife had kicked me out. I asked if the delivery person could climb the shaky trellis in our backyard and bring any food I ordered to the roof. If not, I offered them the use of our trampoline. They said no.

This is what I do with my free time.

I hug everyone. The most awkward moments are when someone goes for the handshake and I go in for the hug, crushing their hand and arm in the process.

126

No one has broken my legs, but I once broke my wrist playing high school basketball. And if that didn't make your enjoyment of this book go through the roof, I don't know what will.

This was a popular strip. I've found over the years that the relatability of a given strip is more important than the quality of the joke. But if you can have both, it's a home run.

127

I see I goofed on this one. Whenever Rat draws the strip, the panel lines he draws are not supposed to be done with a ruler. Instead, they should be hand-drawn and sloppy.

After I submitted this strip, my editor, Reed Jackson, informed me that the Wii was no longer being made. I told him I hadn't kept up with recent gaming news. He replied that it happened seven years ago.

Things got so absurd during the pandemic that people were advocating disinfecting every single product you bought at the grocery store. I remember watching a video of this one guy cleaning each and every package.

130

WHERE'D YOU GO?

TO LOCK MY PHONE IN MY CAR FOR THE NIGHT.

WHAT FOR?

BECAUSE I ALWAYS START LOOKING AT IT BEFORE I GO TO BED. THEN I CAN'T SLEEP BECAUSE I'M TOO NERVOUS AND UPSET.

BUT NOT ANYMORE. BECAUSE I'M FINALLY GOING TO BED AT—

SHOOT. DON'T KNOW WHAT TIME IT IS.

WELL, THAT'S OKAY. I'LL JUST SLEEP 'TIL MY ALARM GOES OFF AT—

DARN... NO ALARM.

OH, THAT DOESN'T MATTER. IF I'M LATE FOR SOMETHING, SOMEONE CAN ALWAYS CALL ME AND—

12/20

NUTS...NO WAY TO REACH ME. THAT MAKES ME NERVOUS.

THAT'S OKAY...I'LL JUST LISTEN TO SOME CALMING MUSIC AND—

As I mentioned earlier, this really was what I was doing with my phone for a while. But we live in an area that has a lot of wildfires, and the only way to know that one's approaching is to keep your phone by you at night.

My editor asked me to mention here that this is dangerous and should not be attempted at home. Though if someone is dumb enough to hit themselves with a mallet, perhaps they have bigger problems.

The year 2020 really was the year of the rat. Fortunately for us, it does not happen again until 2032.

Someday, someone should go through the last 20 or so years of *Pearls* strips and count how many boxes appear. It has to be in the thousands.

Staci truly is in charge of our Christmas cards. Usually, the card will have 20 or so photos of our dog, and sometimes I appear way in the background.

I really do walk around with a baseball cap. But I wear it forward, not backward. Here I am with my best friend Emilio at the Old Absinthe House in New Orleans.

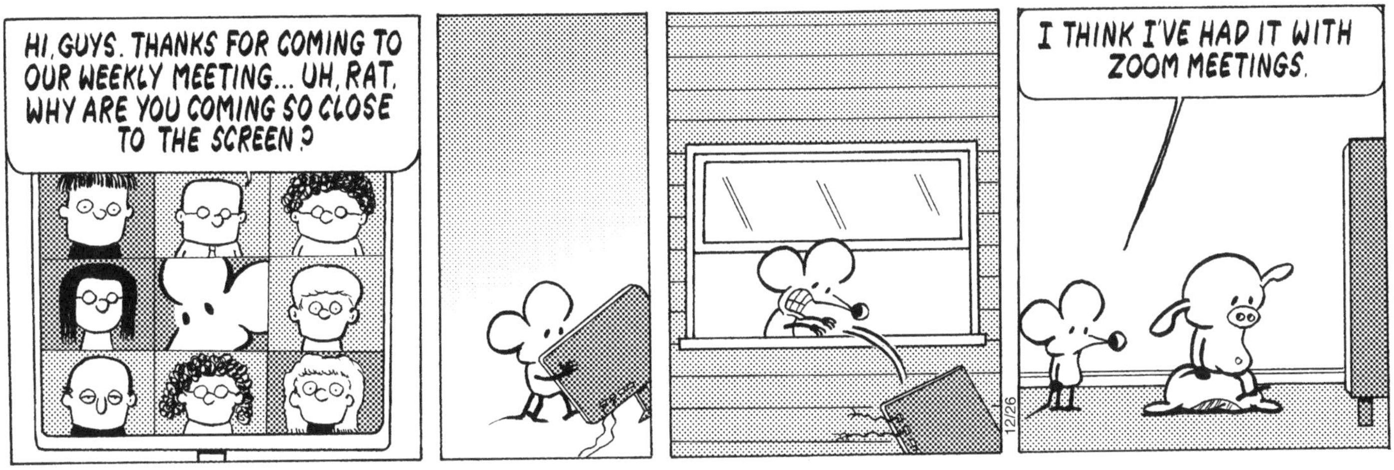
HI, GUYS. THANKS FOR COMING TO OUR WEEKLY MEETING... UH, RAT. WHY ARE YOU COMING SO CLOSE TO THE SCREEN?
12/26
I THINK I'VE HAD IT WITH ZOOM MEETINGS.

Regarding that last comment, I should mention that I once tried ditching the cap for a beanie. It did not go well.

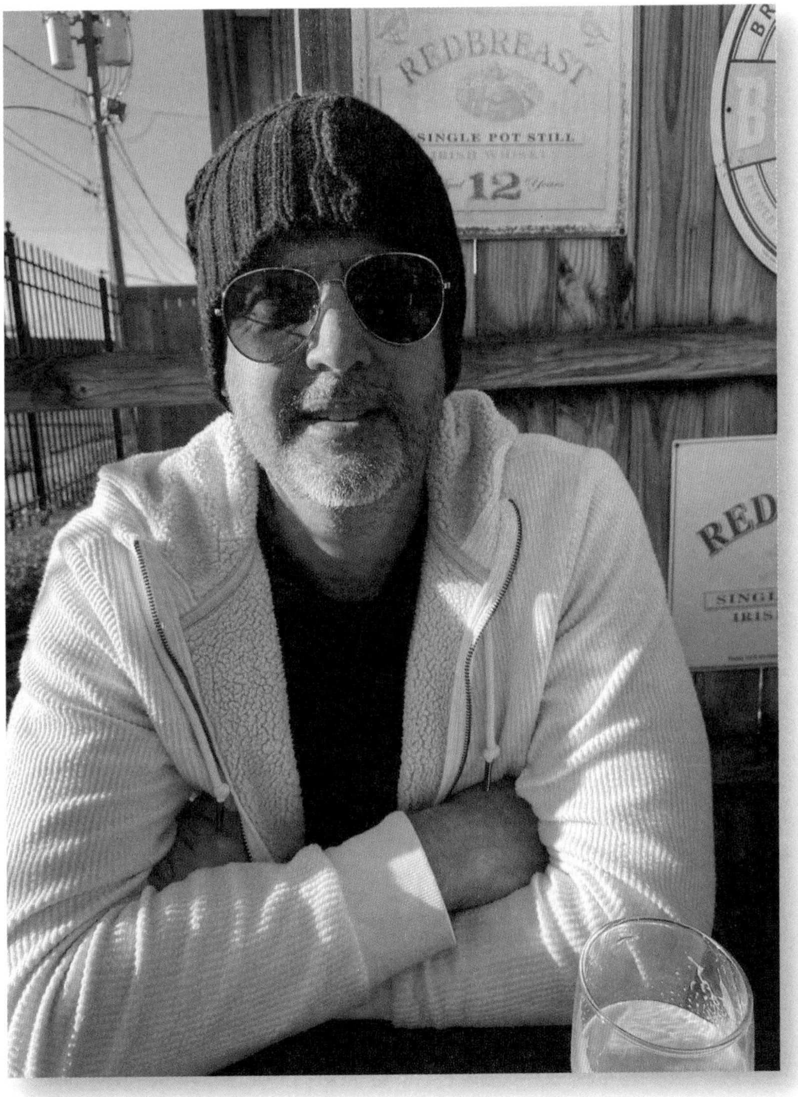
REDBREAST
SINGLE POT STILL
12

I never keep track of what color Rat and Pig's house is supposed to be. Heck, I'm not even sure they live in the same house. Or that they *have* a house. I think the only thing I'm sure of is that I don't look good in a beanie.

I really did get fatter, despite the fact that I started walking 3 miles a day during the pandemic. So I guess that proves walking makes you fatter.

So if I know that the character that talks last in the first panel (Goat) is going to talk first in the last panel, I put the characters at the diner, because I can easily reverse the diner image so that Goat appears first in the final panel. And that, my friends, is the most confusing sentence I've ever written.

This really is my Uber rating. I have friends that are at 4.9 and above, and I have no idea why they are higher than me. Perhaps the drivers rated me based on how I look in a beanie.

Sidenote related to my last comment: I told my former syndicate president John Glynn (Uber rating of 4.91) about the fact that my Uber rating was lower than his and that I needed to catch up. So one day, I ordered an Uber with him in Omaha, Nebraska, and knowing it was MY rating involved, he purposely became very high-maintenance, asking the driver to roll the windows down, roll the windows up, roll the windows down again, etc., all just to tank my rating even further. It was cruel and inhumane.

Pig blew that horn so hard in the third panel that the entire background just disappeared.

Gun-related strips are always risky due to the fact there are so many mass shootings in this country and there's a fair chance the strip will run near in time to one of those tragic events, which will make it look like you're making a joke about it. What a sad reality.

The television in *Pearls* is from sometime in the mid-1970s and is the kind we had in my house when I was growing up. If you wanted to change the channel back then, you had to get up and walk across the room. Unless you were my dad, who just made me do it.

I avoid almost all social gatherings, except the ones my wife, Staci, holds in our own house, which I can't avoid because she won't let me hide in the closet.

Sadly, BIC did not pay me for this fine product placement. I didn't even get one of their cheap, lousy pens. And if they *were* going to send me one, I think I just blew that.

What does "COVID" actually stand for? Now I need to look this up. Answer to come.

HEY, PIG, THIS IS MY FRIEND, LUKE. I ASKED HIM TO COME OVER AND EAT WITH US.

OH, GREAT. YEAH. COME EAT WITH US. AND —

WHAT?

UUUUUSE THE FORKS, LUKE.

THOSE JOKES GET VERY OLD, PIG.

LUKE HOW ANGRY HE'S GETTING.

Note regarding the last comment: Okay, believe it or not, this stupid COVID acronym stands for "**CO**rona**VI**rus **D**isease." So they're just grabbing two letters here, two letters there, one letter here. It is not the way acronyms are supposed to work, and now I'm angry.

IF YOU WORK REALLY HARD, ARE YOU GUARANTEED SUCCESS?

NO.

BUT WHAT IF YOU DON'T WORK HARD? CAN YOU STILL SUCCEED?

I SUPPOSE.

SO BOTH ROADS ARE A CRAPSHOOT. BUT ONE OF THEM INVOLVES GIVING YOURSELF AN ULCER.

LET'S START OVER.

YOU'VE VALIDATED MY LIFE'S CHOICES.

ACME HEALTH. HOW CAN WE HELP YOU?

YEAH, YOU DIDN'T COVER MY LAST DOCTOR BILL BECAUSE IT DIDN'T EXCEED THE DEDUCTIBLE. SO I'M WONDERING WHAT THE DEDUCTIBLE IS.

IT'S VERY EASY TO CALCULATE.

OKAY. HOW?

TAKE WHATEVER AMOUNT YOUR BILL IS AND ADD A DOLLAR.

THAT DOESN'T SEEM FAIR.

DID YOU KNOW 'DEDUCTIBLE' MEANS 'SCREW YOU' IN LATIN?

I believe the same papers that refused to run the earlier strip with the word "turd" in it also refused to run this one. Which is too bad. Because "thankless turd" is a beautiful phrase.

I have a mailbox at the studio where I work, but I've never given the address to anyone, so I know anything sent to it is not something I need. So once every few months, I go to the mailbox, grab the huge stack of stuff inside, and dump it all in the trash. It feels great.

I once stayed in Tucson at a hotel called The Hotel Congress. It's famous because it's where they arrested the gangster John Dillinger in 1934. As a result, he gave them a very poor Yelp review.

145

Note regarding the daily strips from January 18–23, 2021:

If you're one of those strange people who is looking at the dates of the strips in this book (tiny little numbers, usually in the margins), you may notice that an entire week of strips is missing. The book just jumps from one Sunday strip dated January 17 to the next Sunday strip dated January 24. That is because the entire week of strips was pulled from newspapers by my syndicate.

The reason for this was that the strips concerned a violent attempt to remove Rat as President of the United States. And in a ridiculously odd coincidence, real life caught up with fiction on January 6, 2021, when Donald Trump incited a mob to attack the Capitol and try to overturn the result of the 2020 presidential election. Which still feels like a sentence no American should ever have to write.

In any event, my strips were not a comment on that. In fact, some of them had been drawn as early as 2017. But it sure *looked* like I was making light of the tragic events of January 6. I argued that the strips were rather silly and therefore harmless, but with tensions as high as they were, my syndicate thought otherwise. So we compromised by delaying the publication of the strips until August.

As I told one newspaper interviewer: "I think the bottom line is that when you do a series of comic strips about an insurrection in the United States government, you never think there will be an actual insurrection in the United States government."

Below is a panel from one of the strips, which you can see later in this book.

This was one of the most popular strips of the year, and it did not concern a presidential coup, so it could safely run.

NOT A SINGLE THING HAS GONE RIGHT FOR ME TODAY.	SO I'M GONNA GO BACK TO MY BED, WHERE THIS DAY STARTED, AND PRESS THE RESET BUTTON.	NO SUCH BUTTON FOR BAD DAYS.	SURELY THAT'S A DESIGN FLAW.

You may notice there was another gap here. This strip is dated January 28, meaning that the January 25–27 strips are also missing. That is because after the week of coup strips, Larry the Croc became President of the United States. And this second series only made sense if you had seen the prior strips. I tell you, the whole thing was one big mess.

OUR LIBRARY ADDED A WHOLE NEW INDIAN WING. IT HAS INDIAN PROSE AND BOLLYWOOD MOVIES STARRING AAMIR KHAN, SHAH RUKH KHAN AND SALMAN KHAN.	YOU GUYS TALKING ABOUT THE NEW LIBRARY? WHAT DO YOU THINK?	IT HAS PROSE AND KHANS.	NOW YOU CAN BE HATED ON *TWO* CONTINENTS.

I am a big Bollywood fan. If you have never seen one, I suggest you start with *3 Idiots*, which you can usually find on Netflix. It's great.

I JUST DELETED MY FACEBOOK PAGE. I'M DONE WITH THE ARGUING, THE NEGATIVITY, THE UNTRUE STORIES. I CAN'T TAKE IT ANYMORE.		☼CLICK☼	LEMME GUESS. YOU UN-DELETED IT. / DARN THING'S LIKE CRACK.

Sadly, the vaccine people made me wait in line just like everyone else, despite my yelling,
"DON'T YOU KNOW WHO I AM?" repeatedly.

This was another really popular strip. Though you'd have no way to verify that. So I could be lying.

I'm not sure why that bandana on Pig's head has that big bulge at the top. Perhaps that's where he hides his pizza.

In 2020, we finally got solar panels at our house. And when I say "we," I mean my wife, Staci, who contacted the people who do that sort of thing and oversaw the project. My entire contribution to our house is as follows: I eat the food.

150

Some reader commented that Pig's actions here are the textbook definition of chronic depression. I just think he's lazy.

Walter Cronkite was the nightly anchorman on the CBS News from 1962 to 1981, and was famous for signing off each night by saying, "And that's the way it is." I may steal that someday.

As I mentioned earlier, I now walk 3 miles a day. And that's the way it is.

This strip is making fun of the acronym "RINO," which is short for "Republicans in Name Only." And that's the way it is.

My book editor, Lucas Wetzel, has asked me to stop ending each comment with the sentence, "And that's the way it is." And given that he's my editor, I should probably listen.

And that's the way it is.

My niece Elenique (for whom Elly Elephant is named) once made the mistake of giving me the password for one of her streaming subscriptions. I may or may not have been exploiting that password ever since.

154

2/14

This really is a true statistic. Though if you get your facts from me, you're probably doomed.

I'm sort of surprised I got away with this strip, given that it concerns a sexually transmitted disease. But as I see it, I'm educating the youth.

Speaking of lint, we do not have a working washer and dryer at our house. Instead, the washer and dryer are at my studio, a few miles away. So every day or so, Staci gives me a basket of laundry to take with me to work. Which means that as I write these wonderful jokes, I'm also cleaning clothes.

I would now like to change the third panel to: "Invent machine that cleans the clothes at our house, so brilliant Stephan doesn't have to waste his time doing laundry at his studio." Which I can joke about here because Staci doesn't generally read these treasuries.

Note regarding that last comment: After completing this commentary, I forgot what I had written and stupidly gave it to Staci to proofread. She was not happy and asked to type the sentence that appears next:

"Stephan does literally nothing at the house. The least he can do is stick the clothes in the f#$%#$@ washer and press the 'Start' button."

Note regarding the last comment by my potty-mouthed wife, Staci: It is not true that I do nothing at the house. As I stated earlier, I eat the food.

WISE ASS ON THE HILL

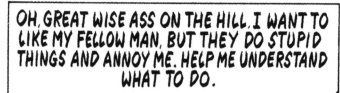

OH, GREAT WISE ASS ON THE HILL, I WANT TO LIKE MY FELLOW MAN, BUT THEY DO STUPID THINGS AND ANNOY ME. HELP ME UNDERSTAND WHAT TO DO.

BEHIND ME IS A GREAT HILL, WHICH IT WILL TAKE MUCH MENTAL AND PHYSICAL FORTITUDE TO ASCEND.

CLIMB THAT HILL, NO MATTER WHAT IT TAKES, UNTIL YOU GET TO THE VERY TOP.

BECAUSE THERE I WILL FIND MY ANSWER?

BECAUSE THERE YOU WILL FIND NO PEOPLE. THEY'RE ANNOYING AS @#☆@.

THE ANSWER IS MORE HILLS.

Ack. The Wise Ass has suddenly gone back to having pointy ears and a long snout. I think it's because this strip is older and was originally set to run in early 2020 but was substituted out to make room for a Covid-related strip.

PEOPLE IN THE GROCERY STORE WHO MAKE THE CHECKER RUN BACK TO THE AISLES TO CHECK A PRICE.

PEOPLE WHO LOOK AT YOU AND ASK IF YOU STILL GO TO THE GYM.

PEOPLE WHO CLAIM TO UNDERSTAND JAMES JOYCE NOVELS.

WHAT ARE YOU GUYS DOING?

DECIDING WHO GETS THE VACCINE LAST.

OOH, CYCLISTS WITH THE TIGHTEST LYCRA.

I vote for the cyclists.

HEY, RAT, DO YOU WANT TO JOIN THE ZOOM PARTY I'M DOING WITH SOME FRIENDS TONIGHT?

WHAT'S THAT?

IT'S WHERE YOU SOCIALIZE ONLINE, BUT IF YOU WANT BEER OR FOOD, YOU OBVIOUSLY HAVE TO BRING IT YOURSELF.

SO YOU'VE ELIMINATED THE TWO BEST PARTS OF A PARTY AND KEPT THE ONE BAD ONE.

SOME PEOPLE DON'T PRIORITIZE FREE BEER.

WE CALL THEM WRONGHEADED.

Sometimes at parties I grab a beer and wander off to the library to stare at the book titles and occasionally even read. For some reason, I rarely get invited back.

HEY, NEIGHBOR BOB, WHAT DO YOU NEED?

WELL, SINCE WE'RE NOW IN A NEW ERA OF TOGETHERNESS, I THOUGHT I'D TRY TO FIND SOME THINGS WE HAVE IN COMMON.

WHITE-HOT HATRED OF EACH OTHER'S POLITICS?

BOB AND I HAVE MORE IN COMMON THAN WE THOUGHT.

159

HEY, NICK, I SEE YOU'RE READING A BOOK ON EUROPEAN ROYAL COURTS.

YEAH, DO YOU KNOW WHAT KIND OF MEN THEY HIRED? I'LL GIVE YOU A HINT— THE MAN WAS CASTRATED.

YOU, NICK?

CORRECT!

THAT'S MORE THAN I WANTED TO KNOW ABOUT NICK.

The joke here is the word "eunuch," which is a castrated man. And you know a joke is good when you have to wait two years for the author to explain it to you in a treasury book.

YOU DOING ANYTHING FOR THE WEEKEND?

I'M HAVING A SOCIALLY-DISTANCED GATHERING WITH MY SIBLINGS.

OH YEAH? HOW FAR DO YOU STAY APART?

TWO THOUSAND MILES.

A BIT FURTHER THAN REQUIRED.

WE'VE FOUND IT WORKS BEST.

One of my sisters recently moved to Idaho, which is more than 600 miles away from me. I would visit her, but the only good stopping point between me and her is a town called Winnemucca, which sounds like a place Winnie the Pooh would go to relieve himself.

Hulloqo zeeba neighba. Peese open door. We is from Federal Department O' Pills. We here give you vaccine pill.

THOSE ARE M & M's. THEY EVEN HAVE THE LITTLE 'M's. ON THEM.

Oh, dat? Dat stand for...

Medeecine.

Moose.

Okay, like, how it be moose?

FIRST WORD COME TO MIND!

My book editor, Lucas Wetzel, informs me that Winnemucca is actually a nice town. So I looked it up and saw that it does have a bunch of casinos. Which is probably why Winnie the Pooh lost all his money and had to live on the streets.

I think I've said it before, but these "Abbott and Costello" routines are by far and away the hardest strips to write. And that's because every single thing the characters say has to have two meanings.

Fun Fact: I showered less during the pandemic than at any point of my life. And if that doesn't make you want to meet me at a book signing, I don't know what will.

On one of my many driving trips during the pandemic, I drove through Fort Worth, Texas, and found the grave of accused Kennedy assassin Lee Harvey Oswald. The strangest part about it was the grave next to it, marked "Nick Beef." The latter grave is reportedly empty. If you're curious, Google "Nick Beef grave."

THE CLOTHING STAGES OF A PANDEMIC

STAGE ONE: SWEATS OKAY FOR WORK ZOOM CALL BECAUSE NO ONE SEES THEM.

STAGE TWO: SWEATS OKAY FOR GROCERY STORE SHOPPING.

STAGE THREE: SWEATS OKAY FOR EVERY SINGLE EVENT IN LIFE.

IS THERE A STAGE FOUR?

SWEATS NEED NEVER BE WASHED.

HEY, NEIGHBOR NICK, I HEAR YOU'RE A BARTENDER NOW.

WRONG. I'M A MIXOLOGIST.

WHAT'S THE DIFFERENCE?

ONE'S A NORMAL GUY AND ONE USES THE WORD 'MIXOLOGIST.'

NO.

ARE YOU THE TYPE WHO SAYS 'PLETHORA' INSTEAD OF 'LOTS'?

I really do avoid any bar where the bartenders are called mixologists, mostly because I know the drinks will be overpriced, and I probably won't like the people drinking them.

HEY, RAT, WHAT ARE YOU DOING?

FINALLY GETTING INOCULATED.

OH, GREAT, SO THAT YOU'RE SAFE FROM THE CORONAVIRUS?

THE ANNOYING EFFECTS OF OTHER PEOPLE.

DIDN'T KNOW THERE WAS A SHOT FOR THAT.

HAHA...LOOK AT THAT GUY DOUBLE-PARKING.

3/7

I am not vain enough to think that other people need to see photos of my food on Instagram. Though I did once take a photo of my right hand and use it to fill an entire page of my last treasury, *Pearls Awaits the Tide*.

The Meaningful Life

Every day, write down one thing you will do to make a difference. And then do it!

I will eat a giant cheeseburger.

And my weight will be different.

CHOMP
CHOMP
CHOMP

Some say the hamburger was invented in Hamburg, Germany. Others say it was invented at a restaurant in New Haven, Connecticut. I say it was invented by Nick Beef.

MY NEW STRATEGY FOR SUCCESS IN LIFE:

DO WHATEVER IT TAKES!*

*Provided it doesn't involve getting up early, effort or sweating.

I HAVE MY LIMITS.

HEY, PIG, YOU SPELLED 'RECEIPT' WRONG THERE. IT'S NOT 'R-E-C-I-E-P-T.'

I CAN NEVER REMEMBER HOW TO SPELL IT.

THIS NEIGHBOR OF MINE IS A TEACHER AND SHE SAYS THE RULE IS 'I BEFORE E EXCEPT AFTER C.'

AND AN ODD RULE LIKE THAT HELPS YOU?

YEAH. IT'S WEIRD SEEING WHAT AN INEFFICIENT SCIENCE THEIR ANCIENT RULES OF GRAMMAR ARE, BUT HIS NEIGHBOR BEING THE PROFICIENT PERSON SHE IS OUTWEIGHS EITHER OF US LIGHTWEIGHTS DISAGREEING.

I SEE WHAT YOU DID THERE.

JUST POINTING OUT FALLACIES.

It really is crazy how many exceptions there are to this rule. I tried to lay out as many of them as I could in that third panel. And for those of you who might not have noticed it, the word "fallacies" in the last panel is another.

165

Ironically, I posted this strip on social media and it was very popular.

I believe we used "Failure is not an option" as a marketing slogan for my middle grade series, *Timmy Failure*. The first book in the series became a Disney movie and can be seen on Disney+.

I actually work six days a week, roughly from 7:30 a.m. to 7:30 p.m. If I do that, I can complete 14 strips a week. That frees up 26 weeks a year to work on other projects, such as the *Timmy Failure* books and the *Trubble Town* books I did recently for Simon & Schuster.

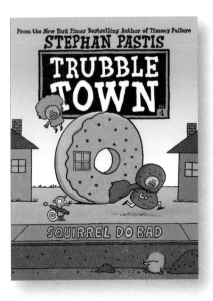

I LOST MY JOB AT THE COFFEE SHOP FOR CONDUCT THAT THEY SAID WAS NOT CONSISTENT WITH THE COMPANY'S VALUES.

WHAT HAPPENED?

OH, YOU KNOW HOW COMPANIES ARE THESE DAYS, SO P.C. AND AFRAID TO OFFEND ANYONE. THEY'LL FIRE YOU FOR THE SLIGHTEST OFFENSE.

WHAT DID YOU DO?

I DIDN'T LIKE A CUSTOMER'S ORDER, SO I HIT HIM IN THE HEAD WITH A COFFEE POT AND KNEED HIM IN THE GROIN.

THEY'LL FIRE YOU FOR ANYTHING THESE DAYS.

AND IT WAS ONLY A FIRST OFFENSE.

Things I've learned in life:

Failure is not an option.

It's a lifestyle.

I'VE DECIDED TO REALLY COMMIT.

HOW WE APPEAR TO OTHERS DURING THE PANDEMIC:

HOW WE SEE OURSELVES:

LET ME OUT! LET ME OUT!

WHERE ARE ALL THE EMPTY WINE BOTTLES?

I KNEW I LEFT SOMETHING OUT.

I think I spent the entire two years of the pandemic in sweatpants. Now when I put on jeans, they suddenly feel confining.

Say it five times fast. (The "bought her better bitter butter batter" part, not the "Surely, your retirement age is nearing" part. The latter of which is hurtful.)

Most people don't know that the First Amendment only applies to the government. It's why a corporation like Twitter can ban whomever and whatever it wants. Which can be a bit scary.

169

HEY, PIG, THANKS FOR PLAYING MINI-GOLF WITH ME.

SURE THING, ANNE. BUT THIS COURSE IS A LITTLE DIFFERENT.

HOW SO?

WELL, THEY TRY TO CONTROL THE PACE AT WHICH PEOPLE PLAY. SO DON'T PUTT UNTIL YOU SEE THAT RED LIGHT FLASH.

OH, AND ROCKS SOMETIMES BLOW ONTO THE COURSE. IN THAT CASE, YOU DON'T HAVE TO PUTT WHEN YOU SEE THE RED LIGHT. YOU CAN WAIT 'TIL SOMEONE CLEARS THEM OFF.

GREAT... SO I'LL JUST WAIT 'TIL THIS RED LIGHT FLASHES.

3/21

NO, NOT HERE.

WHY NOT?

ROCKS, ANNE. YOU DON'T HAVE TO PUTT ON THE RED LIGHT.

THIS MIGHT STING.

DON'T STAND SO CLOSE TO ME.

This was one of the most popular pun strips I've ever done. I never quite know which of these strips will resonate and which won't. I think a lot of it comes down to whether or not people know the underlying song.

Instagram has this relatively new feature called "Reels," which consists of these short videos that I think are meant to compete with TikTok. If I click on it, I find myself watching videos for the next two hours.

Good thing he wasn't up there, because who knows what shape ears he would have.

Or just steal your niece's password. Which I'm not saying I did.

I ended up getting my vaccine shot at a CVS Pharmacy in Healdsburg, California. Which is not particularly compelling, but is the only thing I could think of to say here.

Non-pointed Wise Ass ears. I am relieved.

Fun Fact: When ordering coffee anywhere, I always give my name as "Steve," just so I don't have to spell "Stephan." And that's the kind of insight that makes this book worth every penny.

NOW WHEN THAT GUY SNAPS HIS FINGERS, IT MAKES A CRISP, CLEAR SOUND.

BUT WHEN THAT GUY SNAPS HIS FINGERS, HE CAN BARELY MAKE A SOUND.

WHAT ARE YOU GUYS DOING?

MAKING SNAP JUDGMENTS.

THE SHAME OF THIS STRIP HAS OVERWHELMED ME.

HEY, WHATCHA DOING, PIG?

TRYING TO WRITE PUNS. HERE'S ONE... 'I TENDED A CROWDED BAR.'

WHERE'S THE PUN?

THE WORD 'TENDED.'

THERE'S NO PUN IN THAT WORD.

NO PUN IN 'TENDED'?

YOU MAKE ME DRINK TO EXCESS.

THANKS FOR GOING ON A DATE WITH ME, LULU. TELL ME A LITTLE BIT ABOUT YOURSELF...YOUR LIKES AND DISLIKES.

WELL, I DISLIKE INTOLERANCE, WAR, CRUELTY, SELFISHNESS, GREED, SEXISM, RACISM, LAZINESS, AND STUPIDITY. WHAT ARE YOUR DISLIKES?

PINEAPPLE ON PIZZA.

WE CALLED IT A NIGHT EARLY.

174

Please help this catch on, as I want credit for establishing at least one national holiday.

You know I'm not confident in a joke when I have to make it clear in the fourth panel.

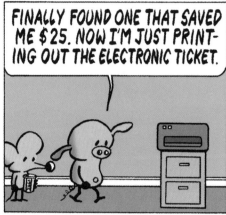

This used to happen to me every time I printed out airplane boarding passes. It drove me nutters.

176

That image of Bob in the second panel is just one I doodled in my notes. And I liked how pathetic he looked, so I just created a strip around it.

I really did read this book. It was so incomprehensible that every time I finished a chapter, I'd look on the internet to find out what had just happened. I'm fairly certain that the only purpose of the book is to make you angry.

OH, GREAT WISE ASS, ALL I DO IS SIT ON MY BUTT WATCHING NETFLIX. WHEN WILL WE FINALLY BE ABLE TO RETURN TO OUR NORMAL LIVES?

WHAT ARE THE THINGS YOU WOULD DO WHEN LIFE WAS NORMAL?

SIT ON MY BUTT WATCHING NETFLIX.

TURNS OUT THAT TO MISS YOUR LIFE, YOU FIRST HAVE TO HAVE ONE.

One of the oddest parts about the lockdown for me was that it didn't look that much different from my normal life. I'm fairly isolated as it is. Which is probably for the best.

WHAT ARE YOU DOING, PIG? — LOOKING FOR A PLACE I CAN RENT ON AIRBNB.

OH YEAH? WHAT TOWN DID YOU PUT IN THE SEARCH FIELD?

'SOMEWHERE THAT IS NOT THE SAME HOUSE I'VE BEEN IN FOR THE LAST 14 MONTHS.'

NOT SURE THAT WORKS. — TURNS OUT IT'S THE MOST POPULAR SEARCH ON THE SITE.

HEY, RAT, WHY IS THE DOOR TO YOUR BASEMENT LOCKED? — WE RENTED IT TO GREG THE GRAMMARIAN.

BUT YOUR BASEMENT DOESN'T HAVE ANY LIGHT OR HEAT.

THAT'S OKAY. GRAMMARIANS JUST NEED DEEP DARK HOLES FROM WHICH THEY CAN JUDGE ALL OF OUR GRAMMARICAL FAILINGS.

'GRAMMATICAL,' MORON. — I JUST DO THAT TO ENRAGE HIM.

I often get emails from people about the grammar in *Pearls*, and so I thought I'd make fun of them by having them live in a dark basement, like a troll or a cockroach. It's nice to always get the last word.

♫ ♪ <u>IMAGINE</u> ♪ ♫

Imagine there's no Facebook
It's easy if you try

No trolls berate us
Around us no more lies

Imagine all the crackpots
silenced for the
daaaaaaaaaaaaaay

Imagine there's no Twitter
It isn't hard to do

Nothing to shill or cry for
And no retweeters too

Imagine all the people
being kind to
youuuuuuuuuuuu

4/11

You may say
I hate screamers
But I'm not
the only one

Who hopes one day
We'll stop this
And the world
will be more fun

Ten months after this strip ran, Facebook's stock plummeted. I believe I am responsible.

The word "alright" is one of their most common complaints. According to them, it is not a proper word. But it's alright with me.

Sometimes I Google "inspirational posters" and just look for ways to make fun of them. Goat's line in the second panel is from one that I saw.

I got through much of UCLA Law School by drawing during class. To the professor, it looked like I was taking notes. But had he seen my "notes," he would have seen that I had just created a rat character that would one day be my ticket out of the law. Here is the page from my class notes where I first drew Rat, at the bottom of which you can see me deciding whether to call him "The Rat" or just "Rat" or "Rat the Rat."

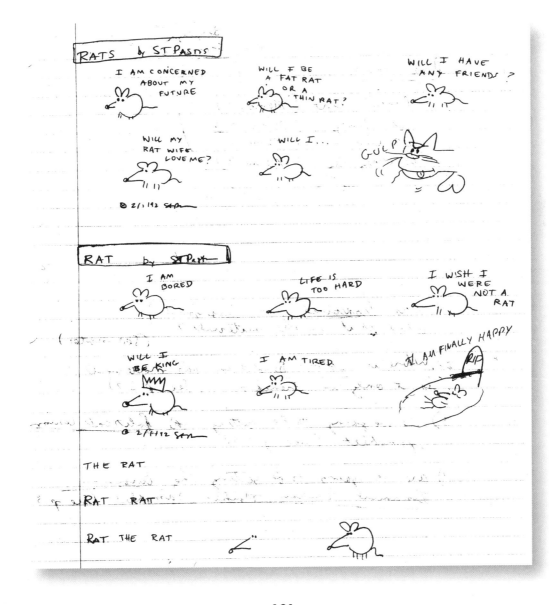

181

> **I'M STARTING TO THINK BUDDHISM MAKES A LOT OF SENSE. FOR EXAMPLE, IT TEACHES THAT DESIRE IS THE ROOT OF SUFFERING. SO TO ELIMINATE SUFFERING, YOU FIRST HAVE TO ELIMINATE DESIRE.**

> **THAT DOES MAKE SENSE.**

> **YEAH. AND HERE I'VE SPENT MY ENTIRE LIFE JUST DESIRING MONEY.**

> **RIGHT. SO WHAT'S THE ANSWER?**

> **SOMEONE WRITING ME A CHECK FOR TEN MILLION DOLLARS.**

> **NO.**

> **OH, NOW YOU'RE SMARTER THAN BUDDHA?**

While in Vietnam in 2018, I got to see one of the world's largest Buddhas. It's hard to get a sense of how large it is from this photo, but I think I would have fit in his nostril.

But far more interesting is this shot from the same trip of me almost being killed by a python. He let me go when I told him who I was.

I think you need to be a little screwed-up-in-the-head to be funny. Thus, I don't go to therapy. Oh, the sacrifices I make.

I just read a study that showed that people who drink two glasses of beer a day live longer. So I assume 10 beers makes you even healthier.

Panel 1: WHAT DOES IT TAKE FOR YOU TO BE HAPPY?

Panel 2: I NEED EVERY SINGLE THING IN MY LIFE TO BE GOING PERFECTLY.

Panel 3: I NEED ONE SLICE OF PIZZA LEFT IN THE BOX.

Panel 4: PIG MAY HAVE AN EASIER TIME. / TWO SLICES AND I WEEP WITH JOY.

Panel 1: DO YOU THINK OUR NEIGHBORS KNOW WE USE THEIR WIFI NETWORKS? / WHY DO YOU ASK?

Panel 2: JUST THE NAMES OF THE NETWORKS.

Panel 3: CHOOSE A NETWORK:

RATSTOPSTEALINGOURWIFI

RATISACHEAP@$$

$#@%#YOURAT

Panel 4: COINCIDENCE.

That is about the closest you can come to saying "cheap ass" on the comics page without actually saying it. The "@" looks like an "a," and the "$" looks like an "s." And while I can say "Wise Ass" (because it's another name for a donkey), I cannot say "cheap ass." (Unless that's a breed I haven't heard of.)

Panel 1: I think my life is about to turn a corner.

Panel 2: GOOD FOR YOU, RAT... WHAT A HOPEFUL ATTITUDE FOR A MONDAY.

Panel 3: Right into an oncoming bus.

Panel 4: THAT'S NOT AS HOPEFUL. / THERE'S NO HOPE ON MONDAYS.

While bored the other day, I found a random bus company online and started messaging them. I asked if on crowded days, I could sit on the roof of the bus if I promised to duck for tunnels. They said no.

Although I try to post strips every day on Facebook, I rarely read people's comments about them. Like a lot of people, I think social media's a real downer, except maybe Instagram, where I can just look at pretty pictures.

We had a big pothole on the street I use to get to my studio, and for the one and only time in my life, I called our city government, who actually sent out a crew to fix it. That and my children are the two biggest accomplishments in my life.

Strangely enough, I relax by reading travel guides for various countries. For me, it's an escape.

I rarely nap. Though my sister Penny naps every day. I am much more ambitious than Penny, and there's nothing she can do to counter that because she does not have access to this commentary.

Regarding that last comment: I just remembered that Penny is an attorney and could view that comment as defamatory. So let me retract it and say she is a wonderful and accomplished person, though probably not above suing her own brother.

Regarding the sister Penny discussion from above: I just gave her a chance to reply to the comments above, and she replied, "Stephan is the smartest of my mother's three children. And it's not even close."

WHAT ARE YOU WRITING, RAT?

PHRASES THAT ARE INCONGRUOUS.

WHATS THAT MEAN?

THEY DON'T SEEM TO GO TOGETHER, LIKE 'FRIENDLY FIRE' OR 'HUMANE EXECUTION.' KNOW WHAT I MEAN?

'URINAL CAKE.'

YOU'VE RUINED LUNCH.

ONLY CAKE I CAN RESIST.

I don't think this item would sell well in bakeries.

HEY, NEIGHBOR NANCY, I WAS WONDERING IF I COULD BUY YOU A CUP OF COFFEE SOME TIME.

SURE. I LOVE VANILLA LATTES. JUST LEAVE IT ON THE FRONT PORCH.

MY PICK-UP LINES ARE NOT AS SUCCESSFUL AS THEY COULD BE.

Dear life,
Every time I do something bad, I regret it afterwards. But it's too late then.

So please invent a type of regret I can feel beforehand.

Call it a 'pregret.'

HOPEFULLY I GET ROYALTIES.

189

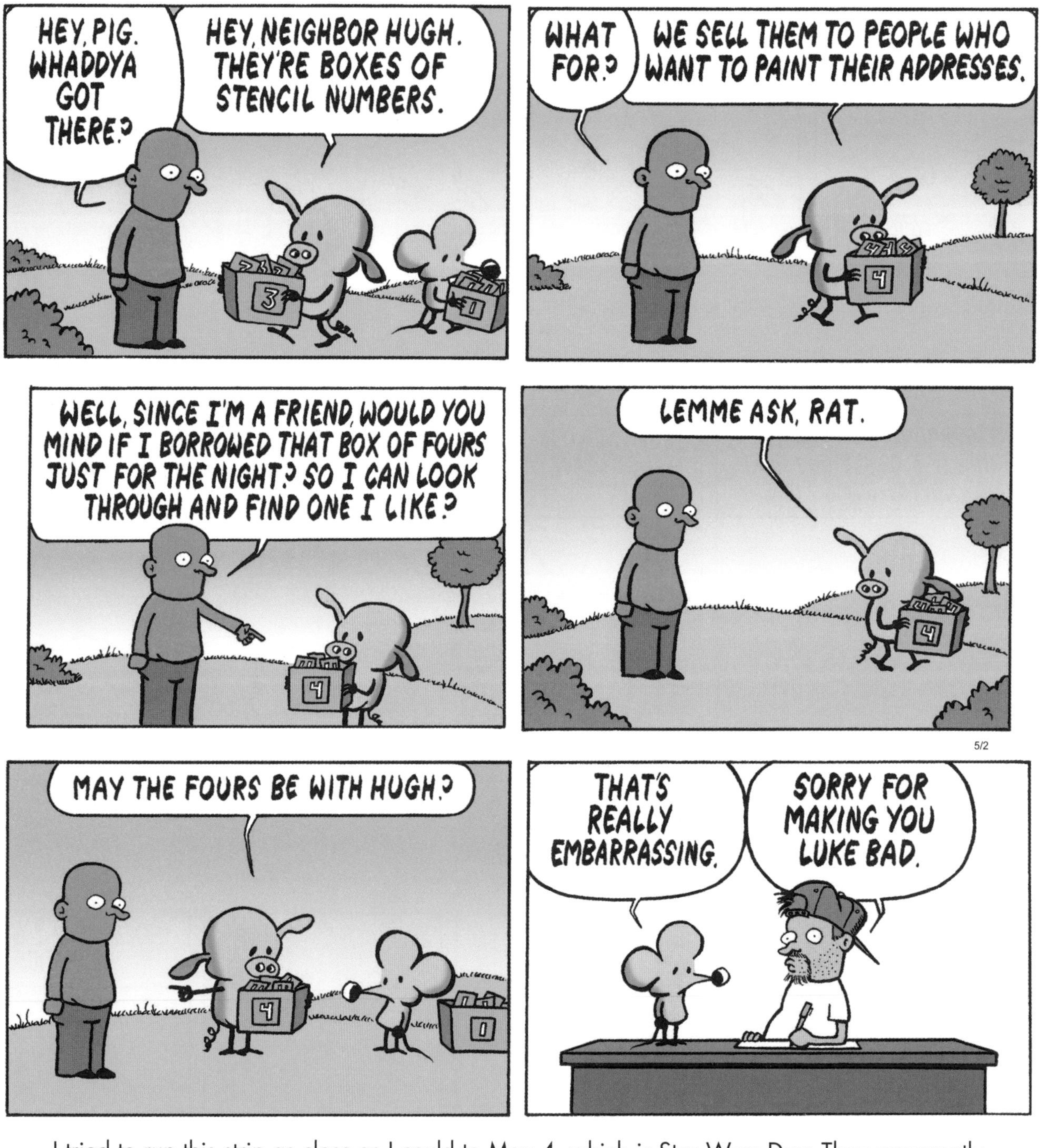
HEY, PIG. WHADDYA GOT THERE?
HEY, NEIGHBOR HUGH. THEY'RE BOXES OF STENCIL NUMBERS.
WHAT FOR?
WE SELL THEM TO PEOPLE WHO WANT TO PAINT THEIR ADDRESSES.
WELL, SINCE I'M A FRIEND, WOULD YOU MIND IF I BORROWED THAT BOX OF FOURS JUST FOR THE NIGHT? SO I CAN LOOK THROUGH AND FIND ONE I LIKE?
LEMME ASK, RAT.
5/2
MAY THE FOURS BE WITH HUGH?
THAT'S REALLY EMBARRASSING.
SORRY FOR MAKING YOU LUKE BAD.

I tried to run this strip as close as I could to May 4, which is Star Wars Day. They apparently chose the date because "May the fourth" is a pun on "May the force."

PIG CAN'T TAKE ALL THE DEPRESSING STORIES IN THE NEWS LATELY, SO HE BOUGHT SOME NOISE-CANCELING HEADPHONES.

I THINK A LOT OF PEOPLE FEEL THAT WAY.

HE'S PRETTY SERIOUS ABOUT IT.

I THOUGHT I RECOGNIZED THOSE TOES.

More from Penny, who saw the quote I attributed to her and just texted me: *"That's not what I said. Also, I have work to do. Actual work. And not whatever it is you do."*

WELCOME, SIR. OUR SPECIALS TONIGHT ARE GRUYERE TUILES WITH DEEP CHEESE FLAVOR AND STEELHEAD TROUT ROE. DO YOU KNOW WHAT YOU'D LIKE TO ORDER?

GIMME FOUR ALL-SEASON TIRES WITH A 30,000 MILE WARRANTY.

MICHELIN STAR RESTAURANTS ARE NOT WHAT YOU'D THINK.

LOOK AT THE HOUSE OF THIS GAMBLER.

NICE.

AND CHECK OUT WHERE THIS BLACK-JACK PLAYER LIVES. AND THIS POKER PLAYER'S FANCY BACKYARD.

DUDE. WHAT KIND OF MAGAZINE ONLY COVERS WHERE GAMBLERS LIVE?

BETTOR HOMES AND GARDENS.

YOU'VE CRAPPED OUT.

While filming the *Timmy Failure* movie in Vancouver, British Columbia, I got a bit inebriated and wandered into a casino, where I played craps. I had no idea what I was doing, but I put down a fair amount of money on something called the "Come" line. The next thing I knew, someone was handing me a whole bunch of chips. Sometimes it pays to be drunk and stupid.

Panel 1: WHICH PIZZA DO YOU THINK WE SHOULD GET? / ARE YOU BEING SERIOUS? YOU GET THAT ONE. IT'S THE ONLY ONE THAT COMES WITH DRINKS.

Panel 2: SIR, THE MARGHERITA PIZZA IS NOT, IN FACT, TOPPED WITH MARGARITAS.

Panel 3: THAT'S VERY MISLEADING.

Surely, I've just given some bar or pizzeria a solid marketing idea here.

Panel 1: HEY, LOOK, WE GOT FORTUNE COOKIES. / MINE SAYS, 'NEXT YEAR BRINGS YOU GREAT SUCCESS.'

Panel 2: HOW NICE. / YEAH, BUT THEY'RE ALL TOO GENERAL AND BLAND LIKE THAT. I'D PREFER SOME SPECIFICITY. READ YOURS.

Panel 3: You will get run over by a 1989 Accord.

Panel 4: SPECIFICITY IS OVERRATED.

There's a place in San Francisco where you can have someone put whatever fortune you want into a fortune cookie. It would be fun to buy one for an unsuspecting friend and have it be ultra-specific to them, like, "Emilio, the right knee you had surgery on in June 1985 will get hurt again when you trip over your dog, Poopy."

Panel 1: PIG'S BUDDY, WILL, GOT THROWN INTO PRISON FOR A CRIME HE DIDN'T COMMIT. / OH, NO. WHAT'S PIG GONNA DO?

Panel 2: TRY TO DRUM UP PUBLIC SUPPORT. BUT I THINK HE'S JUST CONFUSING PEOPLE. / HOW SO?

Panel 3: FREE WILL / MUST BE A PHILOSOPHY MAJOR. / DEEP.

WHEN I USED TO COMMUTE ON THE SUBWAY, THERE WOULD ALWAYS BE THIS ANGRY GUY NEAR THE TICKET BOOTHS.

HE WOULD SHOUT HIS OPINION ON ALL SORTS OF TOPICS. ALWAYS MAD. ALWAYS YELLING.

AND MAYBE SOME OF IT MADE SENSE. OR WAS RIGHT, EVEN. BUT THAT WASN'T THE POINT.

THE POINT WAS THAT I JUST WANTED TO BUY MY TICKET, GET ON THE SUBWAY, AND HAVE A PLEASANT DAY.

BUT THAT GUY KNEW THAT FOR THAT SHORT MOMENT, I HAD NO CHOICE BUT TO LISTEN. SO I DID.

WHERE IS THAT GUY NOW?

IN MY POCKET. ON MY PHONE. EVERY TIME I LOOK AT SOCIAL MEDIA OR THE INTERNET AND LET SOMEONE MAKE MY DAY UNPLEASANT.

BUT NOW I HAVE A CHOICE.

FLING

YOU MIGHT STILL NEED A PHONE.

SAY HELLO TO AN OLD FRIEND.

For the life of me, I cannot draw a rotary telephone. Had cell phones not come along, none of my characters would ever make phone calls.

This could be a big hit. (And that, good reader, is what they call a "bonus pun." Enjoy.)

Awww. A rare, sweet strip designed to trick you into thinking I'm a good person.

This really did generate a whole lot of email, many of which were from cyclists. I think it's safe to say I'm not beloved.

I recently walked into a Ben & Jerry's in New Jersey and somehow got charged nine dollars for an ice cream cone. Maybe the woman behind the counter was a closet cyclist seeking vengeance for her kind.

Speaking of which, if you ever want a signed *Pearls* book, check in with Copperfield's Books in Petaluma, California. They are a great local book chain, and I often drop in to sign books.

As of this writing, the U.S. national debt is 30 trillion dollars. That is roughly equivalent to the number of *Pearls* books sold worldwide.

Note the sad little face on the bin. It's details like this that make me, in the words of *Calvin and Hobbes* creator Bill Watterson, "The best pure artist on the comics page."

Note from Andrews McMeel Publishing's legal department regarding Stephan's 5/17 and 5/18 commentary:

Pearls Before Swine has not sold 30,000,000,000,000 books. Nor did Bill Watterson praise his art skills. As a general rule, Stephan should not be relied upon for factual information.

While weeding in our yard recently, I grabbed what I thought was an orange extension cord that some worker had left in the yard. When I touched it, it moved, as it was not a cord, but an orange-bellied snake. Until that day, I did not know I could leap 10 feet into the air.

Kind of a Corn Flakes–related anecdote: One time in our kitchen, I thought it would be an interesting science experiment to see what kind of sound it would make if I hit my son, Thomas, over the head with a Cheerios box. I don't remember the sound, but I do remember the cereal box exploded and hundreds of Cheerios went everywhere. Thomas didn't even help clean up.

READER ADVISORY:

The content of this strip will be disturbing to some readers.

WHAT'S THE MATTER, PIG?

I HEARD SOMETHING TERRIBLE THIS MORNING. IT RUINED MY WHOLE DAY.

WOULD IT HELP TO TALK ABOUT IT?

I DON'T KNOW.

WELL, TRY.

YEAH. WHAT DID YOU HEAR?

5/23

♬ 1-877-KARS-4-KIDS...THAT'S K-A-R-S, KARS FOR KIDS...1-877-KARS-4-KIDS... ...DONATE YOUR CAR TODAY.. ♬

NOOOO

IT'S STUCK IN MY HEAD FOREVER!

I TRIED TO WARN YOU!

SORRY, EVERY-ONE!

I don't know if this ad runs where you live, but if it does, you know what I'm talking about. Whenever it comes on the TV, I immediately change the channel because otherwise it will be stuck in my head all day.

This really is a common mistake. Or so says the grammarian in his basement.

I'm a "Leave-It-In'er" as well, mostly because I'm too lazy to be a "Pull-It-Out'er." And that sentence seems much dirtier than it is.

The key to a fulfilling life is to take real chances, embrace risk. For we are all too afraid of the unknown.

HEY, PIG, I FORGOT TO ASK....ON YOUR SALAD, DO YOU WANT RANCH OR VINAIGRETTE?

YOU PICK.

THAT WAS EXHILARATING.

I HAVE A NEW MOTTO. WANT TO SEE?

SURE.

Failure is not an option.

THAT'S GREAT.

It's a given.

NEVER MIND.

REMOVES A LOT OF PRESSURE.

I think this is the third time in this book that a strip contains the line: "Failure is not an option." Which I failed to notice.

I DIDN'T ASK TO BE BORN.

I'M A GUEST AT A PARTY I DIDN'T ASK TO COME TO.

AND YET THE TREATMENT OF ME HAS BEEN LESS THAN STELLAR!

IF I'D KNOWN THIS WAS A PARTY, I WOULD'VE DANCED A WHOLE LOT MORE.

Fun Fact: I am not a dancer, but for some reason I made an exception at my niece's recent wedding reception. One person thought I was having a medical emergency.

Around the time this ran, I was driving all around the country trying to talk to people who didn't necessarily think like me. I found that if I treated them with respect and openness, we had more in common than either one of us thought.

I was recently in La Jolla, California, former home of Dr. Seuss, and the spot where the tree that inspired those in *The Lorax* is supposed to be. But when I got there, I discovered that the tree had fallen over and died, much like Dr. Seuss himself.

Sadly, Al Pacino did not write and request the original of this strip. Neither did his brother Cap.

Strange but true: A hole in my sock is so distracting that if I'm writing and I become aware of it, I can no longer write. And that's the kind of person you're dealing with here.

Really, what else does that compliment mean? That said, I do photograph well.

204

HEY, PIG, WHAT ARE YOU DOING?

HAVING A MEETING OF MY SELF-ESTEEM CLUB. WE HELP EACH OTHER GAIN CONFIDENCE.

WELCOME SELF-ESTEEMERS!

WHO'S IN IT?

WELL, MY FRIEND QUINCY, BUT WE CALL HIM 'Q'. WHEN HE ENTERS, WE ALL SHOUT 'RAH' TO CHEER HIM ON.

WELCOME SELF-ESTEEMERS!

THEN THERE'S MY PAL, WILL. HE LIKES TO HEAR PEOPLE SAY 'YES' TO EVERYTHING. BUT HE'S FRENCH, SO WE SAY 'OUI.'

WELCOME SELF-ESTEEMERS!

WELL, IF YOU WANT, I CAN HELP GREET THEM WHEN THEY COME IN. TELL ME AGAIN WHAT WE'LL DO WITH EACH OF THEM.

WELCOME SELF-ESTEEMERS!

6/6

WE WILL 'OUI' WILL, 'RAH' Q.

WELCOME SELF-ESTEEMERS!

YOU SHOULD HAVE NO SELF-ESTEEM AT ALL.

But I *do* have self-esteem. Especially about how well I photograph. Here I am with Abraham Lincoln and his family in Springfield, Illinois. They were great hosts, though a tad stiff.

Fun Fact: If I drink more than one cup of coffee, my right hand shakes just enough that I have trouble drawing the strip. And to those of you who just said, "You mean more trouble drawing than normal?" you're getting a time-out.

Seriously, stop reading the book. You're still in time-out.

Okay, you can start reading again.

DO YOU EVER BECOME CONSCIOUS OF YOUR TONGUE? WHERE IT IS IN YOUR MOUTH? WHAT IT'S DOING? HOW IT FEELS?

NOT REALLY. BUT I AM NOW.

AS ARE MILLIONS OF READERS WHOSE MORNINGS I'VE NOW DERAILED.

THAT SEEMS UNFAIR.

ITH WHY I THON'T READ THE COMICTH THANYMORE.

HA! I had you start reading just in time to see this particular strip so that you would obsess about your tongue for the rest of the day. That's called karma.

I JUST SEEM TO BE GETTING LESS AND LESS PRODUCTIVE WITH MY TIME.

I USED TO BE THAT WAY, TOO. THEN I STARTED DOING VISUALIZATION. YOU JUST VISUALIZE WHATEVER IT IS YOU WANT TO ACHIEVE AND SOMEHOW IT HAPPENS.

WHAT DO YOU LIKE TO VISUALIZE?

NAPPING.

I'M SLIGHTLY MORE AMBITIOUS.

OH, THERE'S YOUR PROBLEM.

Right now I'm visualizing you obsessing about your tongue.

HEY, PIG, DID YOU EVER LOOK INTO HIRING PRIVATE SECURITY TO PROTECT OUR HOUSE? THIS NEIGHBORHOOD IS GETTING TOO DANGEROUS.

YEAH, BUT IT WAS EXPENSIVE, SO I HIRED A GUY WHO WAS A LITTLE CHEAPER.

WHO'D YOU GET?

THE PILLOW MAN FEARS NO ONE.

PERHAPS WE SHOULD SPEND MORE MONEY.

Some days you can't even *find* the idea store.

I really can't see ever retiring. Which is bad news or good news depending on your perspective.

Both my parents are originally from Cleveland. And you're still thinking about your tongue.

I like making Pig almost defy gravity when he's climbing the Wise Ass's hill.

Feel free to insert your own swear words here. For the kids out there, it can be a great language-building exercise.

I'm not as all-knowing as Facebook, but I know that right now a lot of you are reading this book while sitting on a toilet, as many of you tell me that that's where you keep your *Pearls* books. So let me just say for the record—I deserve better.

I wrote this strip after getting on a plane for the first time since the start of the pandemic and being reminded how annoying people could be. The guy in front of me reclined his seat, giving me no room to even cross my legs. All I could think was, "I didn't miss you."

I often ask my mom to admit I'm smarter than both of my siblings. Sadly, she keeps refusing.

There is not one iota of character movement in this strip. I'm proud of that.

Hey, movement in the third panel! This is the closet my strip comes to being action-packed.

Whoa, even more action! We've got sitting, standing, walking, and drinking. You can't ask for more from a comic strip.

HEY, STEPH, THIS IS NEIGHBOR BOB'S KID, JULIA. SHE JUST GRADUATED FROM BERKELEY.

THAT'S GREAT. GOSH, I LOVED MY LAST YEAR AT CAL. THE CAMPUS ACTIVITIES... DRINKING AT 'HENRY'S...'

THE FOOTBALL GAMES WITH AARON RODGERS... BASKETBALL GAMES WITH JASON KIDD... AND GOING TO 'TOP DOG' FOR LATE NIGHT HOT DOGS...

AND JUST GETTING TO KNOW ALL THE OTHER STUDENTS, LIKE AT THE 'DAILY CAL' MEETINGS AND THE PROTESTS WHERE WE OCCUPIED SPROUL HALL.

AND, OF COURSE, GRADUATION AT ZELLERBACH HALL. MY WHOLE FAMILY WAS THERE. NOW HOW ABOUT YOU? HOW'D YOU ENJOY THE EXPERIENCE?

I SAT IN MY BEDROOM AND STARED AT A COMPUTER SCREEN.

MAYBE DON'T REMINISCE AROUND THE COVID GENERATION.

IS SHE STILL CRYING IN THE BATHROOM?

6/27

Fun Fact: NBA Hall of Famer Jason Kidd once played college basketball at my alma mater, the University of California. I wanted to go to his last home game, but it was sold out. So I gave a guard 20 dollars to let me in and found myself standing in the tunnel where the players exit the court. And when Kidd exited, I high-fived him. So if anyone ever asks you who the last person was to high-five Jason Kidd after his last home game, you tell them it was Stephan Pastis.

I'm constantly researching places to go in the U.S., mostly in *Lonely Planet* travel guides and on a great website called Atlas Obscura. When I find a place I want to see, I put a pin in it on my Google Maps app. Here is what my map of the U.S. currently looks like:

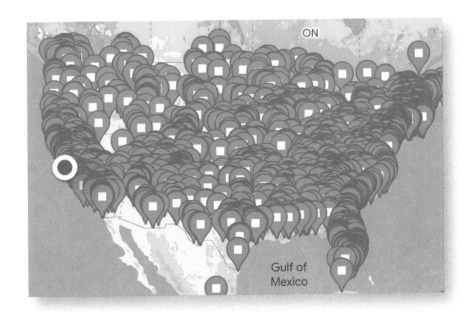

If you think I'm a loon after seeing the map in that last comment, keep in mind that map doesn't even *begin* to show how many pins there really are. For example, here is just New Orleans alone:

If I have a cup of coffee after 6 p.m., I will be up all night. Probably putting pins in maps.

216

I'm hoping that one of you out there will get the "floot floot" line tattooed on your body.
Bonus points if you have it chiseled on your headstone.

Rat's "nasty, brutish, and short" line is from the philosopher Thomas Hobbes. No relation to the stuffed comic strip tiger.

The pandemic was when I started wearing my sweatpants to the grocery store. Though I generally wore a shirt and sometimes even shoes.

I am one of the few people in my family who is not nutters. Except for when it comes to putting pins in maps. Then I'm nutters.

The window in the background is just there to show the passage of time. That's the kind of keen eye for detail I possess. Try to keep up with me if you can.

7/11

Uh-oh. The Wise Ass is back to his old pointy-eared self. Look away if you must.

If you're keeping track at home, that's two straight strips about cheese.

This was a popular strip. But sadly, it ends my cheese streak at two.

While walking the other day, I came across the following sign. I have no idea what it means, other than maybe, "Watch out for random teeter-totters."

I really enjoy drawing Pig when he's happy.

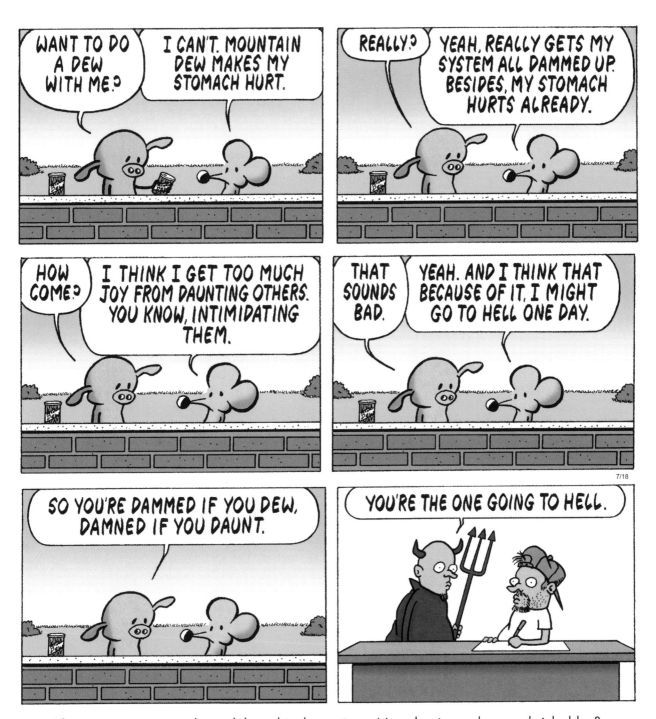

This strip raises some deep philosophical questions. Namely, since when are bricks blue?

Whenever my wife, Staci, tells me to put on something we've recorded on DVR, I act like I don't know what I'm doing and ask her to do it. That's how confident I am she will not read up to this point in the book.

That's a plant on the floor there. It is not a dark cloud hovering just above the flowerpot.

This is what my life will be like if Staci reads that comment from a couple strips ago.

And the "big, long part" is called a bed. Which I know because I just looked it up on Wikipedia.

I was recently in a museum in Philadelphia where I got to see Einstein's brain.
I imagine my brain will one day be put in that same museum so that future
generations can stare at the two great brains of our age.

EMBRACE CHANGE.

NICE.

BECAUSE LIFE GIVES YOU NO ⊙#⊙#*⊙⊙ CHOICE.

LESS NICE.

FROM MY NEW BOOK, "LIFE IS INCONSIDERATE."

Note from Lucas Wetzel, editor of this book, regarding Stephan's prior comment: *I'm putting this note in here after Stephan's final review of this book so that he cannot delete it. But I just have to say that his last comment is indicative of what I'm dealing with when editing his books.*

I JUST TOOK AN I.Q. TEST SO I CAN APPLY TO MENSES.

THE NAME IS MENSA.

DOES THAT MAKE A DIFFERENCE?

YES.

PERHAPS HE SHOULDN'T JOIN MENSA.

WHAT ARE YOU READING, PIG?

A GEOLOGY BOOK. DID YOU KNOW THE CENTER OF THE WORLD IS MOSTLY IRON AND NICKEL?

THAT'S NOT RIGHT.

WHAT DO YOU MEAN?

THE CENTER OF THE WORLD IS ME AND MY FEELINGS.

IT DOESN'T SAY THAT.

I KNOW MORE ABOUT SCIENCE THAN SCIENTISTS.

This is one of my editor Lucas Wetzel's favorite strips. I see Lucas every couple years when I visit the Andrews McMeel offices in Kansas City. I think my visits are one of the highlights of his year.

Note from Lucas Wetzel, editor of this book, regarding Stephan's prior comment: *Untrue.*

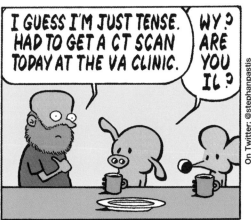

On Twitter: @stephanpastis

Facebook.com/stephanpastis

8/1

The abbreviations here are (1) Hawaii (HI), (2) Alabama (AL), (3) Missouri (MO), (4) Massachusetts (MA), (5) Pennsylvania (PA), (6) Louisiana (LA), (7) Alaska (AK), (8) Maine (ME), (9) Idaho (ID), (10) Oregon (OR), (11) Indiana (IN), (12) Ohio (OH), (13) Maryland (MD), (14) Colorado (CO), (15) Delaware (DE), (16) Oklahoma (OK), (17) Connecticut (CT), (18) Virginia (VA), (19) Wyoming (WY), (20) Illinois (IL), and (21) Georgia (GA).

I just Googled my own net worth. And let me just say—If I had anywhere close to the amount of money listed, I would be on a private island drinking mai tais, and not writing this commentary.

Note regarding that last comment: I just calculated that if every one of you reading this book were to give me an extra $10,000, I could have the amount they say I do. So please consider making a sizable donation.

Oh, the things I get away with. This one was really pushing the limits, at least for newspapers.

True pet peeve of mine. If someone is whistling in a cafe or elevator, I stare at them in disbelief.

8/8

Because Sunday strips have to be submitted at least six weeks before publication, it was really hard timing these pandemic-related ones. I would do a strip like this, and suddenly there would be a renewed surge of the virus, making the strip seem irrelevant.

This is really true for me. I don't even know my best friend Emilio's phone number. Also, when I use the term "best friend," I mean "only friend," as no one else has been foolish enough to befriend me.

In 2020, the fires in my city came within 2 miles of the studio where I draw *Pearls*. As the flames came over the hills, I drove like a maniac from my house to the studio to quickly grab my computer.

Lately, Staci has been making a lot of those mini-crescent dogs. They are those finger-size hot dogs wrapped in a tiny crescent roll. If I eat one, I can't stop. What *will* stop is Staci ever feeding me again if she reads the commentary in this book.

That stupid "thumbs-up" on Facebook Messenger is one of the app's most annoying features, as I somehow keep sending it to friends by accident. One of these days, someone is going to message me that their cat died, and I'm gonna respond with a big thumbs-up.

234

This was one of the most popular strips of the year.

Once again, Pig became a source of optimism in tough times.

It's fun to make fun of health insurance companies, as not one person comes forward to defend them.

236

I still don't understand how Disney could have done this. Both characters are dogs, and yet one has human traits while the other remains a dog. I should introduce a non-talking rat into the strip who just lives in a cage in Rat's house.

It is sort of annoying having the same name as that apéritif, as people are always finding the drink in Europe and asking me if I know about it. I wonder if people ever knock at the door of the company's headquarters and ask if they know about the guy who does stupid puns.

8/22

Kudos to any of you out there who are inspired by this strip to use "Boob" as your coffee name.
I take no responsibility for what happens to you next.

I remember walking mask-less down the sidewalk and seeing a masked person coming the opposite direction who literally jumped off the sidewalk and into the street to avoid me. Although that used to happen to me *before* the pandemic as well.

239

When I went to get the booster recently, I took along my daughter, Julia. I cut ahead of her in line, just in case there was only one dose left.

Pearls Drawing Tip: To change Neighbor Bob into Neighbor Terry, simply add long hair and boobs.

IF WE CAN NO LONGER DO WORK AT HOME, I'M DOING HOME AT WORK.

GOOD NEWS... I NO LONGER HAVE TO DO WORK ANYWHERE.

WELCOME BACK TO THE OFFICE!

You're probably wondering why Pig has a dog, as at no other point in the strip's history has he owned a dog. I do not have a good answer for that, so let me distract you with a photo of my own dog Total meeting a pig.

WHEN YOU'RE YOUNG, YOUR GREAT GRAND-PARENTS DIE, AND YOU'RE SAD. THEN LATER YOUR GRANDPARENTS DIE, AND YOU'RE SAD AGAIN. THEN YOUR PARENTS DIE, AND YOU'RE REALLY SAD.

BUT THEN YOU REACH THIS AGE WHERE DEATH HAS TAKEN ALL OF YOUR FORE-BEARERS, AND THERE'S THIS CALM BECAUSE YOU REALIZE THERE'S NO ONE ELSE IT CAN TAKE FROM YOU.

WHICH IS WHEN IT'S YOUR TURN.

IT'S ALWAYS SOMETHING.

Hey, Junior... Want play game? Me crush you face een Monopoly.

Oh, yeah...You watching TV... You mebbe watch too much. But dat okay. We can watch.

Oh, right. You is playing outside today.

HE KNOWS YOUR SON MOVED AWAY TO SCHOOL, RIGHT?

EMPTY NEST SYNDROME. IT'S REAL.

HAHA..He problee hiding in garage.

There is a major error in this strip. Twenty *Pearls* Points if you can find it.

Answer to question posed in last comment: In the last panel, Larry has not one, but *two* mouths. Somehow that got past both me and my editors.

So this is that week of "coup" strips that was set to run in January of 2021, but was delayed due to the insurrection at the Capitol on January 6. As you can see, they're pretty silly and harmless. But as I said, everyone at my syndicate was worried about running them so near in time to the events of that day.

According to the internet, a Cinnabon Classic Roll has 880 calories, which is almost a third of the recommended total calories a child should eat in a day. So if you're reading this, kids, you need to eat two more of them a day to be healthy.

Strip 1 (9/2):

PRESIDENT RAT IS BEING OUSTED BY A MILITARY COUP.

FINE, FINE, I'LL LEAVE, BUT BEFORE I GO, HOW 'BOUT GIVING ME A PEN SO I CAN WRITE A CONCILIATORY NOTE FOR THE INCOMING PRESIDENT?

SURE.

I HEREBY PARDON MYSELF FOR

I WAS GETTING TO THE CONCILIATORY PART.

Strip 2 (9/3):

WITH PRESIDENT RAT TOPPLED BY A MILITARY COUP, HISTORIANS MOVE TO PRESERVE HIS PRESIDENTIAL PAPERS.

WHERE ARE THEY? IN THIS BOX HERE.

ONE BOX? ONE DOCUMENT.

CRUSH THE LITTLE PEOPLE.

WILL BE HARD TO BUILD A LIBRARY AROUND. OH, AND HE CARVED, "I AM KING" ON THE DESK.

Fun Fact: I have been to the Presidential Libraries of Herbert Hoover, Franklin Roosevelt, Harry Truman, Dwight Eisenhower, John Kennedy, Lyndon Johnson, Richard Nixon, Jimmy Carter, Ronald Reagan, and Bill Clinton. I am only missing those of Gerald Ford and the two Bushes.

Strip 3 (9/4):

AND THEN NEIGHBOR BOB GOES, 'OH, YOU THINK YOU'RE GONNA TOUCH *MY* HEDGES?'

NO HE DIDN'T. I WAS THERE. THOSE AREN'T THE WORDS HE USED, THAT WASN'T HIS TONE, AND YOU LEFT OUT THE RUDE THING THAT *YOU* SAID BEFORE THAT.

YOU'RE RUINING PERFECTLY GOOD GOSSIP.

SORRY FOR THINKING ACCURACY MATTERED. HAVE YOU NEVER GOSSIPED BEFORE? WE SHOULD DISCUSS GOAT WHEN HE LEAVES.

Punching really can be productive. Which is why these books are such a valuable learning resource for children.

I CAN'T BELIEVE I'M NOT PRESIDENT OF THE UNITED STATES ANYMORE.

I DON'T EVEN KNOW WHO REPLACED ME. I MEAN, WITH ALL THAT'S GOING ON IN THIS COUNTRY, WHAT ARE THEIR PRIORITIES?

KEEL zeebas.

This is that second set of strips that got delayed because of the insurrection at the Capitol. Not because there was anything controversial about them, but because they could only run after the week of "coup" strips ran.

LARRY, WHAT TIME ARE YOU COMING HOME TONIGHT?

Late, woomun. Me President of Untied States now.

WHAT DO YOU STILL HAVE TO DO?

Me gotta stop by treasury, get armful of monies.

SIR, THAT'S NOT YOUR MONEY. IT BELONGS TO THE COUNTRY.

Me want quit job.

SIR, CONGRESS HAS PASSED A NEW STIMULUS BILL THAT WILL HELP MILLIONS OF PEOPLE. IT JUST NEEDS YOUR SIGNATURE.

How much zeeba meat me get?

I DON'T BELIEVE IT INCLUDES ANY ZEBRA MEAT FOR THE PRESIDENT OF THE UNITED STATES.

VETO

No wonder everyone hate Congress.

Now that I'm seeing these "Larry as President" strips, I just realized that I never finished the storyline. So I guess Larry is still president. Which might explain much of what is wrong in our country.

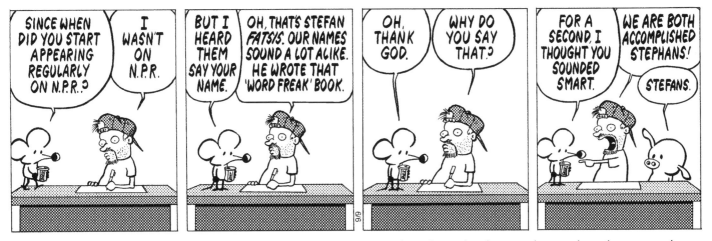

There really is a Stefan Fatsis. And after this ran, we got in touch with each other, and I sent him the original. In return, he sent me a signed *Word Freak* book, which is all about professional Scrabble competitions. It's excellent.

Truly, if you're not paying in some way for local news, your newspaper will go away, and you will eventually find yourself not knowing what's going on where you live. And that's bad.

HEY, PIG, WHAT ARE YOU DOING?

CHECKING IN ALL THESE COUPLES FOR THEIR RECEPTION PARTY. THEY'RE HERE TO GET MARRIED.

WHAT ARE THOSE STARS BY SOME OF THE NAMES ON YOUR CHECK-IN LIST?

THOSE ARE THE ONES WHO'VE ALREADY GOTTEN MARRIED. I'M SUPPOSED TO KEEP A COUNT.

I CAN COUNT THEM IF YOU NEED HELP.

OH, SURE. THANKS.

ONE...TWO... THREE... FOUR.

UH OH. DON'T COUNT THOSE UNMARRIED ONES.

DON'T DO WHAT NOW?

9/12

DON'T COUNT YOUR CHECK-INS BEFORE THEY'RE HITCHED.

COUNT THAT, CARTOON BOY.

Pig's bow ties are much like his regular ties—magically affixed to his body in defiance of all gravitational laws.

Things I look forward to Today:

TRAFFIC!

I'M TRYING TO REVERSE JINX MY LIFE.

Speaking of jinxes, if someone around me says that something good is gonna happen in my life (e.g., "Your book will do great," etc.), I always make them knock on wood three times. My wife, Staci, often refuses, and so I am forced to knock for her.

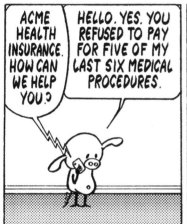

ACME HEALTH INSURANCE. HOW CAN WE HELP YOU?

HELLO. YES. YOU REFUSED TO PAY FOR FIVE OF MY LAST SIX MEDICAL PROCEDURES.

OH, MY. THAT'S NOT GOOD. CAN YOU GIVE US SOME INFORMATION?

SURE.

WHY THE HECK DID WE PAY FOR THAT ONE?

YOU'RE NOT REALLY HELPING.

NO, REALLY. WE'LL FIRE THE GUY.

WHOA. LOOK AT THAT GNU ON NEIGHBOR BOB'S LAWN. AND THERE'S ANOTHER ONE. ARE THEY REAL? BECAUSE IF SO, THAT'S REALLY INCREDIBLE.

FAKE GNUS! SAD.

YOU'RE THE SADDEST PART OF THE COMICS PAGE.

I am not the saddest part of the comics page. That distinction goes to *Family Circus*. Ooh, snap, take that, Jeff Keane.

Note regarding the last comment: My son, Thomas, informs me that no one has said the phrase "Oh, snap" in over 10 years.

When I did this strip, I knew full well that people would write and inform me that the mosquito, and not the hippo, is actually the deadliest animal. But I wanted to leave this strip as is because it was setting up the next day's strip (see below).

So while I was expecting people to write about the fact that hippos were not the deadliest animal, I then made an *actual* mistake in this strip. Ten *Pearls* Points if you know what it is.

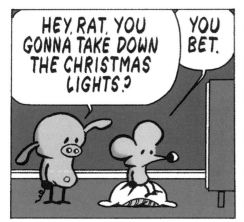

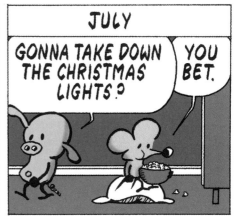

9/19

Answer to question in last comment: The mosquito at the door is male.
But only the female mosquitoes bite.

Fun Fact: Hippos really are the deadliest land mammal, killing roughly 500 people a year. Put that high on the list of things I never want to experience.

I sometimes drop this word into everyday conversation even though I'm not quite sure what it means and am too lazy to look it up.

Spoiler alert: Read these panels in the opposite order that you normally would, starting with the last panel first. But you're smart—So you already knew that. How peripatetic of you.

That is what I would call a peripatetic apology.

9/26

Note from Lucas Wetzel, editor of this book, regarding Stephan's prior comments: *The word "peripatetic" is defined as "traveling from place to place." Stephan is not using the word correctly.*

Sometimes I'd like to kick Lucas Wetzel right in the peripatetics.

I did this strip in response to people who argue that they should be allowed to carry around AR15s, the assault weapon frequently used in many of the nation's mass shootings.

WHERE'S THAT NEIGHBOR WHO WAS SUPPOSED TO COME OVER?

HE'S HEADED DOWNTOWN LATER, SO HE NEEDED TO RUN HOME AND GRAB A MASK.

FOR THE VIRUS, THE SMOKE FROM THE FIRES, OR TO ATTEND A RACIST RALLY?

I SHOULD HAVE ASKED.

YOU HAVE TO BE VERY SPECIFIC NOW.

There were so many fires here in Northern California recently that the skies over San Francisco turned red. Google "San Francisco red skies 2020" to see it. You won't believe it.

WHAT IF THIS WHOLE PANDEMIC THING NEVER ENDS AND WE JUST KEEP GETTING NEW STRAINS OF THE VIRUS?

WHAT ARE YOU DOING?

WELL, NEIGHBOR BOB, I'M AFRAID MY NEGATIVITY BUCKET IS ALREADY FILLED TO THE BRIM THESE DAYS AND JUST CAN'T TAKE ANOTHER DROP. SO, I'M SORRY, BUT...

WHEN YOUR NEGATIVITY BUCKET IS FULL, IT'S FULL.

HEY, NEIGHBOR BOB, HOW ARE YOU DOING?

GOOD. JUST WENT DEER HUNTING.

OH, GOODNESS, I COULD NEVER KILL A LIVING THING.

HOW DO YOU THINK THAT BEEF GOT ON YOUR BURGER?

RONALD McDONALD WAITED PATIENTLY FOR AN OLD COW TO DIE IN HIS SLEEP.

NOT HOW THAT GOES.

AND THE COW HAD ACHIEVED ALL HIS DREAMS AND WAS READY.

When I was a little boy, my Yiayia Pana (*Yiayia* is Greek for "grandmother") used to take me to McDonald's whenever I would visit her house. I would get the Quarter Pounder and she would get the Filet-O-Fish. A child of the Great Depression, she would take all the extra napkins, ketchup packets, and salt packets and put them in her purse to take home. I still miss her.

I draw a lot of balloons and boxes in my strip. Here, my talents are on full display.

The only leadership skill I have is yelling at stupid people. At least I think that's a skill.

I give this strip zero likes because Wise Ass once again has pointy ears. This must have been another strip I drew the prior year.

This may have happened to me.

Whenever Staci stocks the pantry with something really good she knows I will eat, she hides it. And it's a big pantry, so I still have not yet found her hiding spot. But one day I will, and I will gain 45 pounds, and the joke will be on her.

And hopefully, all the wisdom of this book will resonate with you.

Note from Lucas Wetzel:
Whatever.

BONUS SECTION

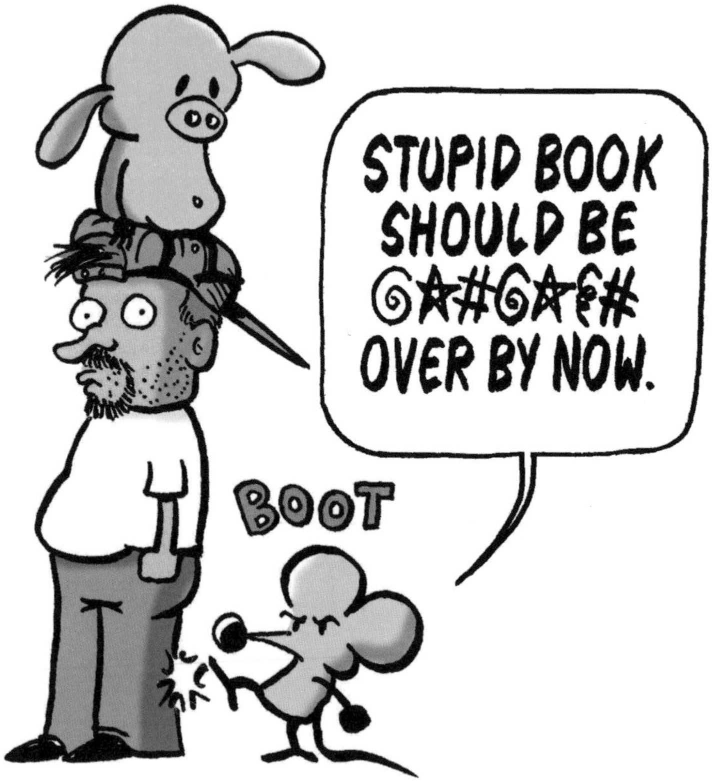
STUPID BOOK SHOULD BE @*#@*&# OVER BY NOW.
BOOT

My editor, Lucas Wetzel—the same guy who enjoys my visits to his Kansas City office and is sometimes too peripatetic for his own good—informs me that we still have an extra three pages to fill in this book.

So I filled one with that "Bonus Section" title page you just saw, one with what I'm typing right now, and one with the image on the page that follows.

I chose the image because I always like to end these treasuries on a heartwarming note. Something to keep you going on the darkest of days.

Enjoy.

Houseplant Baby is watching you.